101 GREAT CHOICES

CHICAGO

Sharon Lloyd Spence

Printed on recyclable paper

PASSPORT BOOKS

a division of *NTC Publishing Group*

Lincolnwood, Illinois USA

Library of Congress Cataloging-in-Publication Data

Spence, Sharon Lloyd.
    101 great choices : Chicago / Sharon Lloyd Spence.
        p.   cm.
    Includes index.
    ISBN 0-8442-8986-8
    1. Chicago (Ill.)--Guidebooks.   I. Title.
F548. 18. S67   1995
917.73' 110443--dc20

                                                    95-14793
                                                       CIP

Cover & interior design by Nick Panos
Cover & interior illustration by Chris Horrie
Special thanks to Sara Schwartz and Karen Ingebretsen
Maps: © MAGELLAN Geographix^{SM} Santa Barbara, CA

1996 Printing

Published by Passport Books, a division of NTC Publishing Group.
© 1995 by NTC Publishing Group, 4255 West Touhy Avenue,
Lincolnwood (Chicago), Illinois 60646-1975 U.S.A.
Manufactured in the United States of America.

   6 7 8 9 ML 0 9 8 7 6 5 4 3 2

Chicago: A Great Choice

I live in Chicago because of Charlton Heston. Ever since I was a small girl, I dreamed of attending Northwesten University so I could study drama and become a world-famous star like its most famous alumnus, Charlton Heston. The first part of my dream came true when I was invited to attend Northwestern's drama school where I happily spent the early 1970s directing and performing in shows including *Waa-Mu*, *The Cherry Orchard*, and *A Funny Thing Happened on the Way to the Forum*. In between theater work, I wrote articles and short stories.

I never did become a star of stage and screen after graduation. Instead I worked my way around Chicago at advertising agencies, public relations firms, and film and video production houses. I also developed severe wanderlust, which is why I now travel the world as a travel writer.

Aside from the time I've spent traveling, I've lived some twenty years in Chicago trying out new restaurants; shopping; exploring museums; and relishing some of the world's best jazz, blues, and classical music. I've also cheered on the Bears, the Bulls, and the Sox and spent thousands of hours riding my bike along beautiful Lake Michigan.

To research *101 Great Choices*, I first compiled my own list of great choices in each category. I then asked for recommendations from editors at the *Chicago Tribune* and the *Chicago Sun-Times*, as well as staffers from the Chicago Office of Tourism and neighborhood development councils. I also received a deluge of phone calls and letters from friends and family who shared their great choices. Many people were generous with ideas and suggestions, and I wish space permitted me to thank each one personally.

Once I had a list of candidates (initially numbering three hundred), I spent weeks making personal visits. Meetings with chefs, shop and gallery owners, museum docents, and sightseeing guides helped me to arrive at the final 101 great choices in this guide.

In each category, I've tried to recommend old favorites and new treasures.

Accommodations range from luxurious five-star hotels to a simple, serene bed and breakfast in the elegant Lincoln Park neighborhood.

Dining choices vary from gourmet cuisine to low-fat lunches for $3.50. You'll find restaurants on busy Michigan Avenue and in Chinatown, Greektown, Little India, Lincoln Park, Andersonville, and on Chicago's South Side. Indulge in some of the world's best seafood, sushi, deli delights, spaghetti, burritos, tapas, ice cream sundaes, vegetarian specials, hamburgers, and, of course, deep dish pizza. There's even a charming restaurant that serves breakfast for breakfast, lunch, and dinner and a coffee shop where world travelers meet and greet.

Entertainment and nightlife suggestions feature theater, music, and dance. Enjoy Chicago's best under the stars beside Lake Michigan; in a smoky, crowded jazz joint; in an intimate art deco piano bar; and in the city's hottest salsa club. Hang out with the beautiful people and sip vodka with Michael Jordan.

There are numerous suggestions for family activities: museums with exhibits for children, museums for kids only, zoos, parks, sports, bus excursions, and walking tours. There's a terrific book-store just for kids, a hamburger diner where waiters dance to Elvis, and an old-style ice cream parlor whose owner calls everyone "honey." For tired parents, there's a quiet library where you can park the kids for a free story hour.

Museums and galleries run the gamut from the known and loved to the less frequented. The renowned Art Institute, Shedd Aquarium, Field Museum of Natural History, and Museum of Science and Industry are on every visitor's list. But save time to explore the DuSable Museum of African-American History, Oriental Museum, Polish Museum of America, Mexican Fine Arts Museum, Chicago Historical Society, and Kohl Children's Museum.

Parks and gardens were easy to find: Chicago's spectacular lake-front parks are well known, loved, and enjoyed. Lincoln Park Conservatory has beautiful, exotic indoor gardens. Check out downtown's newest city garden at Randolph Street and Michigan Avenue, adjacent to the Amoco Building; it's a peaceful oasis amid city bustle.

Making just a few shopping suggestions was difficult because there's nothing you can't find in Chicago's several thousand stores and boutiques. However, we've gone into the neighborhoods to find unique books, one-of-a-kind clothing, handmade papers, trendy western wear, designer duds, gifts for your home, a hip tattoo parlor, and antiques from Thailand.

Sightseeing will take you all over the city, but especially into corners far from downtown. Spend a morning strolling Chicago's historic Pullman neighborhood, hop on a Lake Michigan tour boat for a breathtaking view of the skyline, bask in a sunset panorama from Sears Tower Skydeck 103 stories up.

For sports fans, we've got information on the Bears, the Bulls, the Blackhawks, the Cubs, and the Sox. But did you know about the chic new health club where you can scale a seven-story climbing wall? The new city golf course wedged in between towering skyscrapers? A city scuba shop that guides divers to buried shipwrecks in Lake Michigan?

Those willing to venture outside the city can experience music under the stars at Ravinia, summer home of the Chicago Symphony Orchestra, or a walk through an authentic Japanese garden at Chicago Botanic Gardens.

After months of interviewing people who treasure Chicago, I think my next book might be *101 More Great Choices: Chicago*. With a foreword, perhaps, by the man who helped me fall in love with Chicago, Charlton Heston.

The City at a Glance

Transparency

Getting to Chicago Chicago has two airports: O'Hare International and Midway. A number of airlines offer flights to Chicago, including America West, American, American Eagle, American Trans Air, Air Canada, Continental, Delta, Kiwi, Midway Airlines, Northwest, Southwest, TWA, United, and USAir.

O'Hare is west of downtown on the Kennedy Expressway, I 90-94, at Mannheim Road. On the upper level of each terminal you'll find information booths and stores that sell Chicago maps and guidebooks. The phone number for general airport information is (312) 686-2200.

The cheapest way to get from O'Hare into the city is by Chicago Transit Authority (CTA) Rapid Transit. Catch the train, located under Terminal 4, for a 40-minute trip that costs $1.50 ($1.80 with a transfer). The train runs frequently to and from the Dearborn Street station downtown. From there you can transfer to trains or buses heading north or south.

Continental Air Transport is a convenient bus service from the airport to some thirty-five downtown hotels. Pick up the van outside the baggage claim area. Rates average $13-$20. Call (312) 454-7800.

Other ways to get into the city include taxi or limo services, both of which can be arranged once you arrive. Be sure to negotiate fares before accepting services. Fares range from $25 to $40 one way, plus tip.

Midway Airport, about eight miles southwest of downtown Chicago, is smaller and much less crowded than O'Hare. There are no international flights into this airport.

To get into the city from Midway, you have several choices: taxi, limo, Continental Air Transport (about 40 minutes; fares average $9 to $12), or the Midway Orange Line train. The train runs from about 5 a.m. until 11:30 p.m. for the normal CTA fare of $1.50 or $1.80 with a transfer. Follow the signs to the connecting walkway that takes you to the train, which is just outside the airport. The trip downtown will take about 25 minutes.

Both airports have car rentals, or check with your hotel to see whether it offers a complimentary shuttle from either airport to your hotel. Depending on traffic, the ride will take 45 to 60 minutes.

Getting Around Chicago The grid pattern of Chicago's streets makes it easy to find your way around without getting lost. Lake Michigan is east, and visitors often reorient themselves by asking locals, "Which way is the lake?" The corner of Madison and State streets is the center of the grid: any north, south, east, or west address begins from that point. Each block is equal to one hundred address numbers, so 1000 N. State St. is ten blocks north of Madison. If you can count forward and backward, you can navigate Chicago's streets!

Chicago is a walking city, especially along Michigan Avenue, called the Magnificent Mile. A stroll from the Oak Street beach, to the Art Institute of Chicago on Adams Street would be a fine hour-long walk on a beautiful summer day.

Or you can get around by bus, elevated train (the El), subway, or taxi. The CTA publishes a transit map, available from CTA, Merchandise Mart, Chicago, IL 60654. You can also get free maps and information at Chicago's Visitor Centers: the Chicago Cultural Center, 78 E. Washington St.; telephone (800) 487-2446 or (312) 744-2964. Also at 163 E. Pearson St.; call (312) 467-5307. For transit information by phone, call RTA information at (312) 836-7000. Be sure to know where you are calling from and where you want to go.

Neighborhoods

Away from Michigan Avenue and the Loop are a wealth of ethnic museums, shops, and restaurants from around the world. Here's a brief introduction to Chicago's culturally diverse neighborhoods.

Hyde Park/Beverly/Pullman Historic Neighborhood Hyde Park is home to the University of Chicago, the Oriental Institute, the Museum of Science and Industry, and the DuSable Museum of African-American History. Farther south are lovely, residential Beverly and Pullman, built in the 1880s as a company town for employees of the Pullman Railroad Company.

Near South Side/Chinatown In this neighborhood you'll discover the Illinois Institute of Technology and its Mies van der Rohe buildings. Nearby is the Prairie Avenue Historic District, with the landmark Glessner house and Chicago's oldest building, the Widow Clarke House. Cheer on the White Sox at Comiskey Park. Nearby, Chinatown has superb restaurants and bargain shopping for Asian gifts and crafts.

Printer's Row/Burnham Park Just south of the Loop, this restored neighborhood features top restaurants, clubs, shops, and bookstores. The Spertus Museum of Judaica and Columbia College's Museum of Photography make their homes here. Grant Park has free summertime concerts, and don't miss the Shedd Aquarium, the Adler Planetarium, and the Field Museum of Natural History.

The Loop/Downtown Heart of the city, downtown is home to the Art Institute, Cultural Center, Harold Washington Library, Chicago Symphony, and Lyric Opera. You could spend weeks here, shopping; dining; enjoying theater, music, dance, and views from the Sears Tower Skydeck. Sign up for a guided walking or boat tour with the Chicago Architectural Foundation. Or rent a 45-minute self-guided audio tour for $5 from the Chicago Cultural Center, 78 E. Washington St.

Near West Side/Southwest Side The largely Latino Pilsen neighborhood features the Mexican Museum of Fine Arts as well as wonderful food. Greektown has dozens of superb restaurants, and Little Italy serves up homemade cuisine mostly from the Tuscany region of Italy. The campus of the University of Illinois at Chicago is the site of Jane Addams's Hull House and is surrounded by many renowned medical centers. You can cheer for the Chicago Bulls and Blackhawks at the new United Center.

River North West of Michigan Avenue are renovated warehouse and loft buildings housing art galleries, auction houses, antique stores, jewelers, and trendy clothing and housewares boutiques. Lots of hot nightclubs and new restaurants can be found here, too.

North Michigan Avenue/Streeterville The Magnificent Mile begins here, stretching from Oak Street south to the Chicago River. Look for designer shops, boutiques, major department stores, elegant malls, five-star hotels, fast food joints, and gourmet restaurants. Two excellent art museums are in this area: the Terra Museum of American Art and the Museum of Contemporary Art. Enjoy one of the world's great panoramas from the John Hancock Observatory Deck.

Old Town Beautiful brownstones, quiet tree-lined streets, flourishing flower gardens. In summer there's the Old Town Art Fair. Year-round you'll find excellent boutique shopping along Wells Street, also home to Chicago's comedy mecca, The Second City.

Lincoln Park/Lakeview Visit the Chicago Historical Society, Lincoln Park Zoo, Conservatory, and Chicago Academy of Sciences. Wrigley Field is the ivy-covered home of the Chicago Cubs. Lincoln Avenue features coffee shops, galleries, and unique clothing and gift boutiques. Enjoy Spanish tapas, French crepes, Japanese sushi, homemade Italian ravioli, German brats, Mexican salsa, chocolate fondue, juicy burgers, and deep dish pizza.

DePaul/Clybourn Avenue Look for chic restaurants, top blues clubs, movie theaters, storefront stages, the famous Steppenwolf Theater, and more exciting shops.

Bucktown/Wicker Park Known as a neighborhood of up-and-coming artists, you'll find cutting-edge art galleries, performance art, poetry slams, funky coffeehouses, trendy restaurants, and an international bazaar of craft shops.

Argyle Street/Andersonville At Argyle and Sheridan Road, "Little Asia" serves up cheap and delicious Thai, Vietnamese, and Chinese cuisine. Farther north, on Clark Street, is Andersonville, long home to Scandinavian crafts stores, bakeries, restaurants, and the Swedish American Museum. Newer arrivals include coffee shops for world travelers, books and art by and for women, and several middle eastern restaurants.

Rogers Park/West Ridge From hippie holdouts—the Heartland Cafe and No Exit Coffeehouse—near the lake to a neighborhood of Indian sari shops and restaurants, Jewish bakeries, an Israeli restaurant, and boutiques selling clothes and crafts from Eastern Europe, Russia, and neighboring countries, Rogers Park may be the most cosmopolitan of Chicago neighborhoods.

Weather

The best months to visit Chicago are from May until November. Summers tend to be sunny, with blue skies and cool breezes near the lake. You'll see everyone outdoors biking, jogging, rollerblading, and enjoying the city. From December until April, freezing temperatures, gray skies, and rain and snow can make getting around Chicago less than pleasant, but once you're inside there's lots to keep you busy and happy. Call the daily weather report at (312) 976-1212 for the latest information. Here are Chicago's average temperatures in degrees Fahrenheit:

January—29°	July—85°
February—33°	August—82°
March—44°	September—75°
April—58°	October—64°
May—70°	November—48°
June—79°	December—35°

In summer, shorts and T-shirts are most comfortable. In spring, you'll need a light jacket; for fall, a wool or leather jacket. In winter, from December to March, be prepared to pile on layers of sweaters, a waterproof or snowproof coat, a hat, gloves, a scarf, and waterproof boots.

Banking/Currency

If you are arriving from a foreign country, you may obtain United States dollars at O'Hare International Airport at the currency exchange, which has about forty-five of the major currencies. Hours are 9 a.m.-7:30 p.m. daily, telephone (312) 686-7965.

Another place to exchange currency is American Express at 625 N. Michigan Ave., phone (312) 435-2570; 34 N. Clark St., (312) 263-6617; 122 S. Michigan Ave., (312) 435-2595; and 230 S. Clark St., (312) 629-0685. There are currency exchanges throughout the city; one is Rush Street Currency Exchange, 12 E. Walton St., (312) 337-7117. Open Monday-Saturday, 8 a.m.-10 p.m. Closed Sunday.

Michigan Avenue and LaSalle Street have major world banks, most of which have automated teller machines. Most ATMs belong to the Cirrus network (800) 4-CIRRUS or Plus network (800) THE-PLUS.

If you are sending or receiving money, contact an American Express office, MoneyGram (800-926-9400) or Western Union (800-325-4176).

Sightseeing

Chicago has dozens of sightseeing companies, which will show you the city's best by boat, bus, and on foot. Here are a few to get you started.

BOATS

Chicago Architecture Foundation River Cruises,
May 7-October 31 (312) 922-3432
North Pier Architectural and Historical Cruises,
April 1-October 30 (312) 527-2002
Odyssey Cruises, year round (312)(708) 990-0800
Spirit of Chicago, year round (312) 321-1241
Wendella Sightseeing Boats, April 29-October 7,
(312) 337-1446

BUSES

American Sightseeing Chicago (312) 427-3100
American Tour and Travel/Coach One (312) 978-8900
Chicago Motor Coach Company (312) 922-8919
Gray Line of Chicago (312) 427-3107

Walking Tours

Chicago Architecture Foundation (312) 922-TOUR
Historic Pullman District (312) 785-8181
Frank Lloyd Wright Home/Studio Tours (708) 848-1500
Art Institute of Chicago (312) 443-3600

Tour Guides

Multilingual Ameritours (312) 792-2026
Chicago Tour Company (708) 303-0481
Inlingua International Tours (312) 641-0488

Get more information on sightseeing companies, guides, and special interest tours from the Chicago Office of Tourism (312) 744-2400

Safety/Emergencies

As does any major metropolitan city, Chicago has its share of crime. However, if you stay in well-populated areas of the city and use common sense, you will avoid danger. Here are some tips:

Never walk alone at night anywhere. Take a cab to and from your destination. If you must walk at night in a deserted area, such as a parking lot, go to the nearest police car and ask for an escort. Chicago police will be happy to make sure you stay safe.

Even if you are in crowded areas, avoid petty theft by keeping wallets in front pants pockets and purses securely zipped and worn over the front of the body. Don't carry large amounts of cash or flaunt expensive jewelry. Carry only one credit card and half of your traveler's checks. Leave everything else in your hotel safe.

There is a fair amount of panhandling on Michigan Avenue and on State Street. If you want to make a donation, feel free. If not, avoid eye contact. If you are harassed or followed, go inside the nearest store and ask for help.

If you have a rental car, park only in lots that are well lighted and have security guards. Avoid out-of-the-way lots and self-park lots in which you have to take an elevator or climb stairs alone to get your car.

EMERGENCY INFORMATION

Fire Department 911 for emergency; (312) 347-1313
Police 911 for emergency; (312) 744-4000 for non-emergency
Nursefinders (312) 263-1477
Medical Referral Service (312) 670-2550
Chicago Dental Association (312) 836-7300
Poison Control (800) 942-5969

HOLIDAYS

New Year's Day January 1
Martin Luther King's Birthday third Monday in January
Lincoln's Birthday February 12
President's Day third Monday in February
Memorial Day last Monday in May
Independence Day July 4
Labor Day first Monday in September
Columbus Day second Monday in October
Election Day first Tuesday in November
Veterans Day November 11
Thanksgiving Day fourth Thursday in November
Christmas December 25

How to use this book

101 Great Choices: Chicago is your guide to a sampling of the best that the city has to offer: accommodations, dining, parks & gardens, museums & galleries and other attractions.

If you are interested in a neighborhood-by-neighborhood tour of the city, start with choice no. 1 and wend your way through the book, seeing as much of Chicago as you like, from the Pullman Historic District and Hyde Park to the south, to the Lakefront and Michigan Avenue downtown, and on to the city's North Side. The attractions are grouped into eleven categories, each identified by a small icon at the top of each entry.

If you want to go directly to the best places to eat, shop, take the kids, and so on, use the handy chart below, which lists the attractions in this guide by **category** and **choice number.**

Accommodations
22, 35, 52, 55, 78

Children
3, 4, 28, 45, 70, 74, 79, 101

Dining
8, 13, 16, 18, 34, 39, 41, 46, 49, 56, 57, 59, 61, 62, 66, 68, 75, 77, 80, 83, 86, 87, 88, 90, 91, 94, 98

Entertainment & Nightlife

Miscellany

Museums & Galleries

Out of Town

Parks & Gardens

Shopping

Sightseeing

Sports & Recreation

Chicago and Vicinity

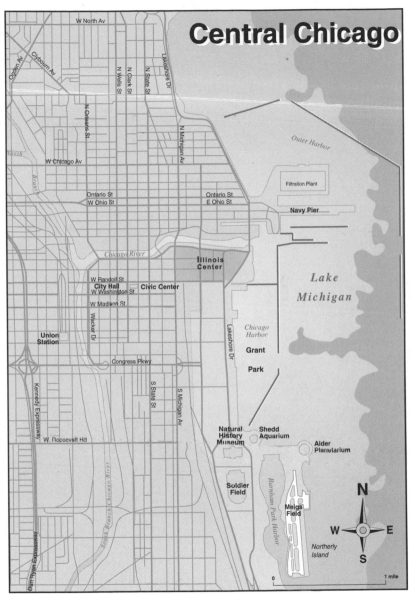

Central Chicago

W North Av

Ogden Av

Clybourn Av

N Orleans St

N Wells St

N Clark St

N State St

Lakeshore Dr

N Michigan Av

W Chicago Av

North

Branch

Ontario St
W Ohio St

Ontario St
E Ohio St

Outer Harbor

Filtration Plant

Navy Pier

Chicago River

Illinois Center

W Randolf St

City Hall
W Washington St

Civic Center

W Madison St

Wacker Dr

Lake Michigan

Union Station

Congress Pkwy

Kennedy Expressway

S State St

S Michigan Av

Lakeshore Dr

Chicago Harbor

Grant

Park

W. Roosevelt Rd

Natural History Museum

Shedd Aquarium

Alder Planetarium

Soldier Field

Burnham Park Harbor

Meigs Field

Northerly Island

South Branch Chicago River

Dan Ryan Expressway

N

W   E

S

0   1 mile

Downtown Chicago

101
GREAT
CHOICES
CHICAGO

Sharon Lloyd Spence

1 / Self-guided Walks through a Historic Town

Pullman Historic District

"We struck because we had no hope," cries Jenny Curtis, a seamstress who worked for the Pullman Palace Car Company in 1894. "My rent to the company was $7 and my salary a mere $10 per month. What else could I do but strike?"

Step back 100 years to Chicago's Pullman neighborhood, "America's most perfect town." George Pullman built homes, shops, even a church for the 14,000 workers who manufactured his luxurious railroad cars. Houses had indoor plumbing, running water, garbage collection, and landscape maintenance.

Life was fine for a time. The neighborhood had Greek, Italian, and Polish grocery stores where workers could buy food from their homelands and converse in native languages. Pullman had stables, a beautiful park, and a hospital. Everyone lived in a home owned by Pullman. All of life's needs were met.

All of life's needs—except the opportunity to buy one's home or to save for a future outside Pullman. By summer of 1894, Pullman workers had formed a local branch of the American Railway Union and struck, protesting wage cuts and oppressive company practices. The strike escalated into a national railway workers' boycott. President Grover Cleveland intervened, and 12,000 federal troops were deployed to break the boycott. Pullman workers were forced back to work on the company's terms.

A number of Pullman homes have been restored. Guided walking tours are conducted the first Sunday of each month at 12:30 p.m. and 1:30 p.m. from May to October; self-guided walking tours are permitted any time. Pullman's story comes alive through reenactments in which actors portray striking workers. "Join us," says Jenny Curtis.   *Out of Town/South*

Pullman Historic District For schedules and information, contact Historic Pullman Foundation at the Visitor Center, 11141 S. Cottage Grove Ave., Chicago, IL 60628; (312) 785-8181. Guided walking tours: $2.50-$4. Private homes open the second weekend in October.

2 / Romantic Restaurant in an 1881 Queen Anne Hotel

Hotel Florence

Wealthy travelers in George Pullman's railroad cars enjoyed unusual amenities for the 1880s: elegant furnishings, gleaming woodwork, elaborate fixtures, attentive service, and five-star cuisine.

Today the elegance of a bygone era thrives at the Hotel Florence, an 1881 showplace where Mr. Pullman entertained clients. The red-brick Queen Anne-style hotel, named for Pullman's favorite daughter, is now a restaurant, museum, and romantic setting for weddings and fundraisers. Even Hollywood has discovered Pullman, using the town as a setting for *The Untouchables* and *The Fugitive*.

Meals are served in the airy forest-green parlor room, decorated with lace curtains, a pressed-tin ceiling, and ornate wall sconces or in the dining room, where gleaming cherry paneling and stained-glass windows set a more formal tone.

The hotel serves lunch from 11 a.m. until 1 p.m. Monday through Saturday, breakfast from 9 a.m. until 1 p.m. on Saturday, and an all-you-can-eat Sunday brunch.

Mr. Pullman forbade his workers to drink at the Hotel Florence bar, but visitors are welcome to enjoy a cold refreshment at The Brass Tapper down the hall from the dining room. The hotel gift shop offers books, cards, T-shirts, and Pullman train memorabilia.

The parlor rooms upstairs—where Mr. Pullman entertained the Marshall Fields, the Potter Palmers, and Abraham Lincoln's son Robert Todd (who became the Pullman Company's second president)—are much like they were in 1881. Mr. Lincoln's portrait hangs respectfully beside Mr. Pullman's massive handcarved mahogany bed as though the two gentlemen may one day dine again at the magnificent Hotel Florence.

Out of Town/South

Hotel Florence, 11111 S. Forrestville Ave., Chicago, IL 60628; (312) 785-8181. Sunday brunch, $8.95. Free parking.

3 / Zoo With African Wildlife Habitats

Brookfield Zoo

Go on safari into a five-acre African reserve called Makundi National Park. "Makundi" is Swahili for "a gathering place for people or animals." Brookfield Zoo's new "Habitat Africa" exhibit features African wild dogs, dwarf mongooses, klipspringer antelope, and gray-headed kingfishers. Majestic reticulated giraffes browse the outdoor waterhole alongside Grant's gazelles and ostriches.

If you love dolphins, catch their show at the "Seven Seas Panorama Dolphinarium," complete with tropical plants and an underwater viewing gallery. Outside, wander rocky shores of the Pacific Northwest, home to sea lions, walruses, and seals. At "The Fragile Kingdom," visit an African desert and an Asian rainforest. Outdoors are Siberian tigers, snow leopards, and jaguars. At "Tropic World," a pathway overlooks gorillas, monkeys, and free-flying tropical birds amid waterfalls and towering forests.

At the children's zoo, watch chicks hatch, pet a horse, and learn how cows are milked.

The zoo covers 215 acres, so a good way to get started is to see the orientation program in the Discovery Center, then take the "Motor Safari" tram to the exhibits that interest you most. In June there's a birthday party for Affie the African Elephant, and in December the zoo hosts a Holiday Magic Festival. Special events are held every month, so call for dates. The zoo has 3 restaurants, 11 snack stands, 4 gift shops, a bookstore, and plenty of souvenirs for everyone. Wheelchair, wagon, and stroller rentals are available.

Out of Town/Southwest

Brookfield Zoo, 14 miles west of downtown Chicago, at First Ave. and 31st St., Brookfield, IL 60513; (708) 485-0263. Open 365 days a year, Memorial Day-Labor Day 9:30 a.m.-5:30 p.m.; Labor Day-Memorial Day 10:00 a.m.-4:30 p.m. Parking is $4. Admission $.75-$4; children under 3 are free.

4 / Aquarium Featuring Innovative Whale and Dolphin Exhibits

The Shedd Aquarium

"If there is magic on this planet," said naturalist Loren Eisley, "it is contained in water."

Enter the underwater world of the Shedd Aquarium, a mesmerizing universe of whales, sea otters, penguins, sharks, eels, turtles, and fish from all corners of the world. Dim, mysterious galleries contain marine animals from the Caribbean, the Indo-Pacific, the cold oceans, the Great Lakes, and the tropics.

Several times daily, a diver plunges into the 90,000-gallon Coral Reef to chat with viewers while feeding sea turtles, nurse sharks, moray eels, and hundreds of rainbow-hued fish. Each year, Shedd scientists return from diving expeditions with new specimens, such as pygmy angelfish, blackcap basslets, copper sweepers, and warty anemones.

The Oceanarium's trails wind through a Pacific Northwest forest. Whales, dolphins, sea otters, and harbor seals frolic in shimmering three-million-gallon pools. Huge underwater windows on the lower level make close-up viewing easy, as belugas flirt and float serenely by. On penguin shores, comical birds cavort and waddle over rocky terrain.

Several times a year the Shedd invites parents and kids to bring their sleeping bags for an overnight adventure. Evening activities, snacks, and a late-night feeding at the coral reef are followed by a morning wakeup with the whales.

The Soundings Restaurant is a good choice for lunch, and several gift shops offer marine souvenirs, toys, gifts, and books.

Near South Side

The Shedd Aquarium, 1200 S. Lake Shore Dr., Chicago, IL 60603; (312) 939-2438. Hours: 9 a.m.-6 p.m. Open 7 days a week; closed Christmas and New Year's Day. Admission: $3-$8.

5 / Natural History Museum of Dinosaurs and World Cultures

Field Museum of Natural History

Explore an Egyptian tomb, venture among the peoples of the Northwest and Arctic coasts, stroll on a Pacific beach, or watch a fiery lava flow. Meet villagers of Senegal, Cameroon, and Zaire, who share techniques and technologies that Africans brought to the Americas.

Even in a lifetime you'd never see everything at this vast museum. The world-renowned collection spans nine acres, but exhibits just a few of the museum's nineteen million artifacts.

The Field Museum of Natural History was founded in 1893 to house the natural history collections gathered for the Columbian Exposition. The original museum opened its doors in 1894 and moved to its present building in 1921.

Today the Field Museum is one of Chicago's treasures, unveiling innovative exhibits that draw visitors back again and again. Two of the newest are "Live Over Time: DNA to Dinosaurs" and "What Is an Animal?"

"Live Over Time" takes you through 3.8 billion years of life's history, a world of 400-million-year-old nautiloids, monstrous millipedes, dimetrodons, and, of course, dinosaurs. From the time of the dinosaurs, journey through the Ice Age, mammal and human evolution, and into the future of life on Earth.

"What Is an Animal?" challenges visitors to explore the surprising scope and diversity of the animal kingdom. Get a new perspective on where animals live and how their color, shape, and size help them survive.

Although you can never see all of the Field Museum in a lifetime, you can have fun trying.

Near South Side

Field Museum of Natural History, E. Roosevelt Rd. and S. Lake Shore Dr., Chicago, IL 60605. Hours: 9 a.m.-5 p.m. daily; closed Thanksgiving, Christmas, and New Year's Day; (312) 922-9410. Admission $3-$5. Wheelchair accessible.

6 / Sports Stadium for the Chicago Bears

Soldier Field

Great events often happen simultaneously. In 1922 construction began on Soldier Field, and at the same time George Halas, founder of the American Professional Football Association, which later became the NFL, renamed his football franchise the Chicago Bears.

The Bears began playing in Soldier Field in 1971, defeating the Pittsburgh Steelers 17-15 before a crowd of 57,000. Today the team is still fighting it out from August to December for fans who love them whether they win or lose. Football lovers know there's nothing like bundling up on a cold Sunday afternoon with 66,000 other Bears fans, cheering the team in one of the world's most ornate stadiums.

Soldier Field, which cost $13 million, was originally built as a memorial to American soldiers who died in war. Designed by architects Holabird and Roche in the style of ancient Greek and Roman stadiums, it's graced with classic Doric colonnades rising 100 feet above the playing field. The first event in 1925 featured 1,000 police athletes, followed by the 1926 Army-Navy game and the renowned 1927 Jack Dempsey/Gene Tunney heavyweight rematch. Over 100,000 visitors turned out in 1944 to hear President Franklin Roosevelt and in 1962 to hear evangelist Billy Graham.

Since those early days, Soldier Field has presented rodeos, tractor pulls, rock concerts, fireworks displays, stock car races, marching bands, operas, and even a ski jump. In 1994 the stadium hosted the opening ceremonies and several games of the World Cup Soccer tournament.

Near South Side

Soldier Field, 425 E. McFetridge Dr., Chicago, IL 60605. For schedule of events call (312) 294-2200. For Bears tickets call (708) 615-2327. For information on Bears trips, parties, and events, call (800) 790-BEAR.

7 / Hands-on Science Museum for Techno-buffs

Museum of Science and Industry

No matter how much energy the family starts out with, there's no way to see this whole museum in one day. Spanning fourteen acres, one of Chicago's most beloved museums houses more than 2,000 exhibits. So you'll have to make some tough choices.

One of the newest exhibits, "Kids' Stairway: A Child's Path to Self Discovery," helps youngsters get in touch with their feelings, raising their self-esteem and giving them new information on the dangers of drug and alcohol abuse.

The Henry Crown Space Center is very popular, with spaceships, lunar models, and moon rocks chronicling our explorations of outer space. A spectacular domed Omnimax Theatre shows larger-than-life films on sharks, sports, and wilderness adventures.

The museum has a sixteen-foot-high pulsing heart, eggs hatching into chicks, and a WW II vintage U-505 submarine. An HH-52A helicopter hangs suspended over a coal mine, where an elevator descends into darkness. Secrets of the human brain are unlocked at "Learning and Learning Disabilities: Explorations of the Human Brain."

The museum's striking classical architecture dates back to its construction as part of the 1893 Columbian Exposition. Julius Rosenwald, Chairman of Sears, donated $7.5 million to have the building refurbished in the 1920s. It opened as the Museum of Science and Industry in 1933. Today it welcomes over two million visitors a year. Special events are scheduled monthly and include "Black Creativity," the "Hispanic Festival," and "Christmas Around the World." *Near South Side*

Museum of Science and Industry, 57th St. and S. Lake Shore Dr., Chicago, IL 60637; (312) 684-1414. Hours: Memorial Day-Labor Day and holiday season 9:30 a.m.-5:30 p.m.; other times—Monday-Friday 9:30 a.m.-4 p.m.; Saturday, Sunday, and holidays 9:30 a.m.-5:30 p.m. Admission: $2-$5. Children under 5 free. Thursdays free. Wheelchair accessible.

8 / Italian Café near Famous Chicago Museums

Piccolo Mondo

Customers seated at sunny window tables with views of Hyde Park's lush green trees buzz with conversation. Professors and doctors from the nearby University of Chicago talk philosophy and medical research. Grandparents gush over new photos of their grandchildren. Tourists get their second wind after a morning at the Museum of Science and Industry or DuSable Museum of African-American History.

"Many of our customers eat here every day," says manager Norberto Zas, "because our food is very fresh—fish, vegetables, pasta; even our herbs are grown here in Hyde Park."

La caprese salad tastes just picked: slices of juicy tomato nestle with fresh creamy mozzarella, drizzled with virgin olive oil and topped with basil leaves. Homemade spaghetti with fresh calamari, shrimp, mussels, clams, and scallops is tasty. Other choices might be panni, an Italian sub sandwich made with provolone cheese, prosciutto, fried eggplant, or meatballs. Bigger appetites enjoy chicken vesuvio—a half chicken roasted in rosemary and wine sauce, or the veal scaloppine—slices of veal sautéed in white wine and mushrooms, served with a brown sauce.

Service is relaxed and pleasant, as most of the staff have been a part of the Piccolo Mondo family for many years. Manager Zas drifts among the twenty-three tables exuding Italian-Argentinean charm, catering to his loyal but demanding customers. "Europeans come for pasta with olive oil and basil, Asians want fresh seafood, tourists like fresh sandwiches. Everyone has a different taste. We work hard to keep them all happy."

Near South Side

Piccolo Mondo, 1642 E. 56th St., Chicago, IL 60637; (312) 643-1106. Monday-Thursday 11:30 a.m.-8:30 p.m., Friday-Saturday 11:30 a.m.-9:30 p.m., Sunday 3-8:30 p.m. Italian deli carry-out is also available.

9 / Museum Showcasing African American History, Art, Culture

DuSable Museum of African-American History

A newspaper advertisement in the 1839 *Cincinnati Gazette* proudly proclaims that "swelled rail bedsteads by Henry Boyd are warranted to be the best and most convenient beds ever made."

Henry Boyd, once a slave in Ohio, became a successful furniture manufacturer, earning a reputation for creating magnificent four-poster beds. But his success was hard won: Mr. Boyd's factory was burned down three times. Three times Mr. Boyd rebuilt his factory, refusing to let "minor obstacles" stand in his way.

The DuSable Museum honors African Americans like Henry Boyd who overcame barriers. Oil portraits and bronze statues in the museum's Halls of Fame honor many African American heroes: poet and author Langston Hughes; orator Sojourner Truth; slave abolitionist and American statesman Frederick Douglass; athlete, actor, and lawyer Paul Robeson; Harriet Tubman, known as the "Moses of Her People."

Permanent and changing exhibits are diverse: a recent one featured altars of the Yoruba, Kongo, Shang, and Omolo peoples in Africa. Another exhibit featured Dr. Carter G. Woodson, the founder of Negro History Week, lauding his "successful effort to mobilize a racial minority through historical consciousness."

The DuSable Museum has a lively year-round calendar of events: films, lectures, conferences, music, dance, arts and crafts, and children's programs. The museum gift shop carries Kenyan fertility dolls, Nigerian kufi hats in colorful kente cloth, and books by notable African American authors.

Near South Side

DuSable Museum of African-American History, 740 E. 56th Pl., Chicago, IL 60637; (312) 947-0600. Hours: Monday-Thursday 10 a.m.-6 p.m.; Friday 10 a.m.-5 p.m., Sunday and holidays noon-5 p.m. Admission: $1-$3; kids under 6 are free.

10 / Dramatic Museum of Near East History, Art, Archaeology

Oriental Institute Museum

"Trusting in the support of the great gods, I went to and fro. The peoples from the upper Bitter Sea to the lower Bitter Sea I brought under one rule. From Egypt to Mushki I brought them in submission to my feet."

Those were the self-congratulatory words of Sargon, King of Assyria in the 8th century B.C., a conqueror who gradually took control of Mesopotamia, western Iran, and Syria. This legendary ruler established the Akkadian dynasty, a kingdom that ruled for almost 2,000 years. Now that's power.

Welcome to the Oriental Institute Museum, a showcase of the history, art, and archaeology of the ancient Near East. Founded in 1919 by James Henry Breasted, the institute has sponsored projects in the Nile Valley, Mesopotamia, Persia, and the Ottoman Empire.

The Oriental Institute Museum has a fascinating collection of antiquities from temples, private houses, and tombs of ancient Egypt, Iran, Iraq, Israel, Syria, and Turkey. What the museum does so well is present the fascinating personalities who lived and ruled from 3500 B.C. to A.D. 100, as well as the important historic events. In the museum's five galleries you'll discover the origins of agriculture; the invention of writing; the birth of cities; and the beginning of our endeavors in the arts, sciences, politics, and religion.

Meet your fellow Sumerians, Assyrians, Babylonians, and Persians at the Oriental Museum and see how very little—or very much—life has changed these past 5,495 years.

Near South Side

Oriental Institute Museum, 1155 E. 58th St., Chicago, IL 60637; (312) 702-9520. Hours: Tuesday 10 a.m.-4 p.m., Wednesday 10 a.m.-8:30 p.m., Thursday-Saturday 10 a.m.-4 p.m., Sunday noon-4 p.m. Free admission.

11 / Bookstore Specializing in Humanities, Social Sciences

Seminary Co-op Bookstore

No cute tables for sipping fresh-brewed cappuccino or munching on poppyseed muffins. No windows or plants. The black painted concrete floor has worn away where book lovers have shuffled up and down narrow, overflowing aisles since 1961, searching for books they can't find elsewhere.

The Seminary Co-op Bookstore of Hyde Park specializes in academic books in the humanities and social sciences. There are over 100,000 titles, mostly from the major university presses, independent scholarly publishers, and literary houses.

Books, stacked higher than your head and lower than your ankles, cover every shelf and table in rooms curving out of sight. The Co-op is a sacred catacomb of words, unveiling secrets of poetry, philosophy, history, economics, and science. Readers explore foreign horizons, guided by the *Critical Dictionary of the French Revolution*, *The Search for Modern China*, and Wole Soyinka's *Art, Dialogue and Outrage*.

Nobody here complains about the glaring fluorescent lights or exposed water pipes and electric wires. Classical music plays softly from a tiny, black boom box. People stagger under armloads of books. Women wearing packs on their backs and babies on their hips compare book lists; bearded men with thick glasses stand engrossed reading *Civilization of the Mind*.

For a few minutes, put aside all thoughts of cookbooks, science fiction, who-done-its, romance, and sports. Nourish your mind with brain food from the Co-op Bookstore.

Near South Side

Seminary Co-op Bookstore, 5757 S. University Ave., Chicago, IL 60637; (312) 752-4381. Hours: Monday-Friday 8:30 a.m.-9 p.m., Saturday 10 a.m. -6 p.m., Sunday noon-6 p.m. Members receive a 10 percent discount.

12 / New Home of the Chicago White Sox

Comiskey Park

Opened in April of 1991, Comiskey Park is the country club of stadiums: 3,400 royal blue bleacher seats are comfortable, the field is as green as Ireland, and 2,500 people are at your service. That's right—by the time you add up the ushers, the clean-up crew, the food vendors, and the security folks, there's a small town making sure you have a great time at Comiskey Park.

Some fans have too much fun. When Sox first baseman Frank Thomas recently hit a home run in the second inning, one fan leaned out of his seat to catch the ball. He somersaulted forward out of his seat and flipped eight feet down onto the ground! The park paramedics rushed him to first aid for a check-up, pronounced him completely unhurt, and sent the guy back to his seat thirty minutes later.

Even if you're not a fan, the perks here are pretty spiffy. The press room is decorated like a *Fortune* 500 executive office, with 120 fancy chairs and hookups for each reporter's private phone and computer. Corporate suites are even posher, with plush upholstered couches, bars, kitchenettes, and windows that open to the field, just in case some big cheese actually wants to hear the crowd roar.

The grass at Comiskey Park gets four-star treatment. Head groundskeeper, Roger Bossard, makes sure his playing field is cut, combed, and watered daily. Most pet dogs don't get that kind of care. Mr. Bossard even created a drainage system so that, if it rains, the field is dry in forty-five minutes.

The April-October season features eighty-one home games, and tickets are available in advance by phone or on game day at the box office. So grab a cold beer and let's play ball.

Near South Side

Comiskey Park, 333 W. 35th St., Chicago, IL 60616; (312) 924-1000. Wheelchair-accessible seating.

13 / Unusual Cantonese Cuisine in Chinatown

Emperor's Choice

"We enjoy explaining our Cantonese dishes and introducing guests to new tastes," says co-owner Pat Moy, who opened the restaurant in 1988 to raves that have continued ever since. When was the last time you sampled sea cucumber, fish lips, and black mushroom casserole or peasant's abalone with goose web? These dishes are just a few of Emperor's Choice Village Specials, which the menu suggests "may need an acquired taste."

Of course there are the standard favorites: hot and sour soup—a thick hearty blend of tofu, bamboo shoots, shredded pork, bean cake, and mushrooms, with a dash of vinegar and chili pepper. There's kung bao chicken—chunks of tender white meat and peanuts in a peppery chili-tomato sauce. And oceans of fresh seafood, shrimp, lobster, sole, clams, oysters, and shark's fin soup.

Speaking of those tiny green chilies: they're not as innocent as they look. A customer once swallowed one and flew out the door looking for the Chicago Fire Department. Pat calmed her down and fed her steamed white rice, and minutes later she was again enjoying her meal. *Take note:* Another customer stops in weekly, ordering Pat's giant Olympian oysters and Chinese spinach. She then mixes everything together to create "Oysters Rockefeller," Chinese style. "We like her innovation," laughs Pat.

Emperor's Choice has a relaxing decor of forest green, beige, and burgundy walls sporting framed ink-on-silk portraits of emperors of China's ten dynasties. Outside, the 1930s building features authentic Chinese statues that ensure gastronomic happiness to all those who enter.

Near South Side

Emperor's Choice, 2238 S. Wentworth Ave., Chicago, IL 60616; (312) 225-8800. Hours: Monday-Saturday 11:45 a.m.-12:30 a.m., Sunday 11:45 a.m.-11:30 p.m. Entrées from $7.50 to $19.95.

14 / Museum of Mexican Painting, Sculpture, Photography, Textiles

Mexican Fine Arts Center Museum

Discover a rich variety of visual and performing arts from Mexican and Latino cultures. Since its Pilsen neighborhood opening in 1986, this innovative museum has established a world-wide reputation for creative exhibits and fruitful exchanges between the United States and Mexico. In 1992 the Museum signed a "sister museum" agreement with El Museo del Templo Mayor in Mexico City to exchange resources, exhibits, and staff. In 1993 the museum unveiled the work of twenty contemporary Mexican artists in "The Art of the Other Mexico," to travel throughout the United States and Mexico. The permanent collection consists of over 800 works of art by Mexican and Mexican American artists.

A recent exhibit featured one of Mexico's national treasures, sculptor Juan Soriano. This exhibit presented not only the sculptor's art but huge color photos of Soriano at work. A videotape of Soriano and portraits of him by well-known photographers all contribute to a satisfying total picture of the artist as man, the man as artist.

Celebrating the Pilsen neighborhood, another exhibit featured photos taken by children of Orozco Elementary School. Another room presented the work of young artists from Chicago and Mexico City, who have participated in an exchange program titled "Sin Fronteras" ("Without Walls").

The Mexican Fine Arts Center has received many awards for its extensive educational arts programs for children, teachers, and schools; has hosted Mexican performers, Latino theater companies, and avant-garde arts events; and has received accolades for its Day of the Dead exhibition, the largest in the nation.

Near West Side

Mexican Fine Arts Center Museum, 1852 W. 19th St., Chicago, IL 60608; (312) 738-1503. Hours: Tuesday-Sunday 10 a.m.-5 p.m. Free admission.

15 / State-of-the-Art Sports, Music, Theater Arena

United Center

The Chicago Bulls and the Chicago Blackhawks have a new $175-million-dollar home. The sports palace has 950,000 square feet of flash and dash, accommodating 21,500 Bulls fans and 20,500 Blackhawks fans in plush theater-style seats.

The octagonal scoreboard alone cost $6 million, weighs 50,000 pounds, and glows with 178,000 light bulbs. "This is by far the biggest indoor electronic information board we've made or we know of," says Jim Wood, vice president of Chicago's White Way Signs. "It's got everything: instant-replay screens, myriad basketball statistics, lights, and size. It will bring the fans closer to the game."

The organ is state of the art, and has three keyboards, each with sixty-one keys and computer-generated instrument sounds. The custom-built organ uses sound sampling, a technology that records and electronically plays back tones. Over 100 switches enable the organ to generate sounds from 60 instruments.

There are forty-six concession stands dishing up fajitas, quesadillas, and frozen margaritas, in addition to the standard hot dog and fries; a sportswear and souvenir store called "Fandemonium"; and a seventy-seat "Hall of Fame Theater" showing highlight films of sporting events.

The United Center will also stage boxing and wrestling matches, concerts, and shows such as "Disney's Aladdin on Ice," Aerosmith concerts, and the Barnum & Bailey Circus.

For anyone who ever waited in long lines to use the washroom, take comfort: United Center has 48 public rest rooms.

Near West Side

United Center, 1901 W. Madison St., Chicago, IL 60607; (312) 455-4500; box office at Gate 4, open 11 a.m.-6 p.m. daily, 11 a.m.-8 p.m. on days of events.

16 / Delicious Greek Food with Family-friendly Service

Greek Islands Restaurant

Three businessmen stride into Halsted Street's Greek Islands Restaurant. "Peter, how ya doing?" they ask, shaking the manager's hand like long-lost friends. "Where ya gonna seat us today?"

"About 80 percent of our customers are regulars," acknowledges Peter Thaniotis, who came from Sparta twenty-three years ago to Greek Islands Chicago, working his way up from busboy to general manager. "They're here for lunch during the week, then bring their friends and families back on the weekend."

Cheery blue-and-white checked tablecloths, giant sacks of garlic cloves, and fanciful murals of Greek fishing villages create an appropriate backdrop for the food to come. First arrives complimentary taramosalata, a creamy, salty, pink fish-roe spread, delicious on soft fresh bread. Saganaki is next, flaming Kefalotiri cheese with lemon, oozing onto the plate in a hot chewy pool.

Favorite entrées from chef Pete Kappos include pastichio—macaroni with layers of ground beef, cream sauce, and tomatoes; lamb ami fournou—pan-roasted lamb with olive oil, lemon, and oregano; fresh red snapper and sea bass; chicken riganati, chicken baked with oregano and garlic; and meatballs with basil and mint.

The menu promises to "be kind to your arteries" with home-made desserts without butter, low in cholesterol. But Greek Islands's "special dessert" is decadent, a sweet syrupy mixture of filo crust, lemon custard, almonds, walnuts, and whipped cream. Greek nogatina is a refreshing blend of walnuts, almond cake, and orange-peel cream.

Be sure to ask Peter about his home town of Sparta, where Greek Islands gets its tasty olives, olive oil, and wine.

Near West Side

Greek Islands Restaurant, 200 S. Halsted St., Chicago, IL 60661; (312) 782-9855. Hours: Sunday-Thursday 11 a.m.-midnight, Friday-Saturday 11 a.m.-1 a.m. Daily specials average $7.50. Free valet parking.

17 / One of the Oldest and Largest Ethnic Museums in the U.S.

The Polish Museum of America

One of the oldest and largest ethnic museums in the United States is in a magnificent ballroom where 2,000 people once danced. Everything in this delightful museum, founded in 1935, celebrates the accomplishments of the Polish people.

There's the elegant bronze sculpture of Maria Sklodowska Curie, the Polish-born French physicist we know as Madame Curie, who twice received the Nobel Prize for her work on radioactivity and the discovery of radium and polonium.

There's General Casimir Pulaski, "Father of the American Cavalry," who marched into South Carolina during the Revolutionary War, in defense of Charleston and Savannah, where he was mortally wounded. President Herbert Hoover honored the general by proclaiming October 5 "Pulaski Day."

Madame Helena Modrzejewska is featured in all her theatrical glory. The great Shakespearean actress starred in *Twelfth Night* to great acclaim in the late 1800s. She also performed in Henrik Ibsen's first American production of *A Doll's House*.

Polish and Polish-American paintings, sculpture, drawings, and lithographs are dramatically displayed, as are military regalia, church relics, native folk costumes, hand-painted Easter eggs, ornate jewelry, and a magnificent stained-glass window.

The gift shop has an excellent collection of dolls in native costumes, jewelry boxes, hand-carved wooden plates, Baltic amber jewelry, and Polish cookbooks.

The museum is a fascinating place to learn how the Poles advanced science, enriched the arts, and changed the course of history.

Near West Side

The Polish Museum of America, 984 N. Milwaukee Ave., Chicago, IL 60622; (312) 384-3352. Free admission; free parking. Hours: 11 a.m.-4 p.m. daily.

18 / Where Cops, Politicians, and Ordinary Citizens Dine on Gargantuan Deli Fare

Manny's Coffee Shop and Deli

I always know when my husband, filmmaker Warren Lieb, has eaten at Manny's. "I had hot pastrami today," he confesses, avoiding my eyes.

"What else?" I ask.

"Gefilte fish, matzo ball soup, potato pancakes."

"And?"

"Baked apple."

"I'm not cooking dinner tonight."

"Fine. I'm not hungry either."

Of course he's not hungry either! Manny's pastrami sandwiches are huge, a half slab of meat and bread that barely fits into a wide-open mouth. The matzo ball soup is so rich with chicken fat that your arteries harden just thinking about it. Potato pancakes, served with sour cream, stick to your thighs as well as your ribs. Baked apples? OK, they're light. Still, forget dinner.

Daily specials at Manny's are legendary and include baked whitefish, stuffed cabbage, braised tongue, stuffed veal breast, fried smelt, and gefilte fish—among many others. Manny's offers 8-10 hot entrées daily, so plan your tour schedule accordingly.

Manny's has been south of Chicago's Loop for 31 years, a family-run cafeteria in which neighbors greet Ken Raskin (the late Manny's son) and Arlene, Ken's mother, by name. Chef Eleanor Shelli keeps most of the incredible recipes in her head.

Meanwhile, my husband stays slim and healthy on his generally low-calorie, low-fat diet. But when he heads for Manny's, even I can't save him.

Near West Side

Manny's Coffee Shop and Deli, 1141 S. Jefferson St., Chicago, IL 60607; (312) 929-2855. Hours: Monday-Saturday 5 a.m.-4 p.m.; closed Rosh Hashanah and Yom Kippur. Entrée prices range from $3.25-$7.30.

19 / Explore Beautiful Parks and Beaches along Lake Michigan

Chicago's Lakefront

Chicago's lakefront is an oasis of emerald parkland, curving bike paths, beaches, and recreational facilities on Lake Michigan. The lake may be crashing thunderously on the beach or as calm as a sleeping kitten. Like a chameleon, its colors change hourly.

By car, start south of the city at Soldier Field. From Lake Shore Drive looking north, the skyline view is fantastic: The Planetarium, the Shedd Aquarium, the harbor overflowing with million-dollar party yachts. Driving north around the Shedd, the panorama looms closer: Sears Tower, the John Hancock building, and a wall of other brick, glass, and stone monoliths.

Continuing north, Buckingham Fountain appears on the west, rainbow-hued sailboats on the east. Pass the Grant Park bandshell, where summer visitors are treated to free concerts.

As you cross the Chicago River, the glittering mirrored skyline is west and Lake Michigan stretches east to forever. At Navy Pier, the new Skyline Stage looks like a wild mushroom.

Vintage and contemporary residences line Lake Shore Drive. At Fullerton, exit to Lincoln Park Zoo and the Conservatory, a few blocks west. At Belmont, exit, park in the nearby lot, and ride a bike north past the harbor, the beach where dogs frolic, and up Recreation Drive to an Indian totem pole. You'll find public tennis courts as well as a public golf course. At the Irving Park exit, there's a playground for kids cooped up in the car too long.

From the pier at the Montrose exit you'll find a favorite lakefront vista. Head east onto the wide boulevard and right again at the Park Bait Shop. Look east for a blue-and-white beach house. Turn left onto the paved pathway that leads to a beachside parking lot. A concrete pier curves out into Lake Michigan like a question mark. Surrounded by sea gulls, the moody lake, and a peaceful sandy beach, few city views in the world rival this. And admission is free.

Michigan Avenue/Lake Shore Drive

20 / Canoe or Hike along the Chicago River

Friends of the Chicago River

"Lake Michigan is our majestic front door," says David Jones, Deputy Director of the Illinois Department of Energy and Natural Resources. "But our back door, the Chicago River, is what's historically significant to the city's development. One hundred fifty years ago the river was the busiest port in North America, as boats exported grain out from the prairie, and imported textiles, farm tools, and European immigrants back into the prairie. Chicago became a huge metropolis because of the Chicago River."

For over fourteen years, Mr. Jones has been a docent with Friends of the Chicago River, a nonprofit organization that "embraces the river as part of our culture, economy, and natural heritage and works to improve the environmental quality of the Chicago River."

To educate people on the unique aspects of the river, the organization sponsors walking tours and canoe trips from May to October. Urban adventures range from exploring the river's quiet wooded wilderness on the North Branch to the industrial scene of Goose Island and the rich architectural history of the river's Main Branch. The Upper North Branch makes a dramatic transition from forest preserve to urban residential neighborhoods. In August canoes float under a full moon, stopping for dinner by lantern on an island in the Skokie Lagoons.

"Our walking and canoe tours delight people by taking them places they'd be unlikely to find by themselves," says Mr. Jones. "Even most native Chicagoans don't know about them."

Michigan Avenue/South Loop

Friends of the Chicago River, 407 S. Dearborn St., Suite 1580, Chicago, IL 60605; (312) 939-0490. Tours range from $5 to $35.

21 / A New Music Center for Instruments, Gifts, Sheet Music

The Chicago Music Mart at DePaul Center

Strolling past the Music Mart around noon, you may hear Dave Brubeck's "Take Five," Debussy's "L'Isle Joyeuse," or Chopin's "B-Flat Minor Scherzo." It's all part of the Music Mart's free "Tunes at Noon" concerts, presented every weekday from noon to 1 p.m. Bring along a sandwich or just relax and enjoy.

During the early and mid-1900s, Chicago's music row along South Wabash Avenue was home to a variety of music manufacturers and retailers. The first American-made harp was produced in this neighborhood by Lyon and Healy, as were the upright and player pianos. Thomas Edison's gramophone was also introduced in this area.

Today the historic building has been renovated and reborn as a shopping emporium dedicated exclusively to music, musical instruments, and musical gifts. Some of the companies in the building include Baldwin Piano and Organ, Carl Fischer Music, Keyboard World, and Musical Threads.

Soundproof rooms in the Music Mart enable musicians to "test drive" an instrument in private.

Stop by for the free noon concerts. Whether you favor classical music or contemporary tunes, you'll be in happy company with other music lovers.

Michigan Avenue/South Loop

The Chicago Music Mart at DePaul Center, 333 S. State St., Chicago, IL 60604; (312) 362-6700. "Tunes at Noon," weekdays noon to 1 p.m.

22 / A Sleek Celebrity Hotel with a Superb Downtown Location

Chicago Hilton and Towers

On any Monday or Wednesday evening dozens of beauty queens may be roaming the hotel lobby. The Luvabulls, the Chicago Bulls' cheerleading squad, rehearse here. Upstairs in a lavish suite, Scottie Pippen was videotaped in bed for the local TV talk show "Fox Thing in the Morning." Harrison Ford hung precariously from the rooftop balcony in a scene from *The Fugitive*. Liza Minnelli often stays here, as does Eddie Murphy.

The location is superb, within easy walking distance to the Art Institute, Shedd Aquarium, Field Museum, Goodman Theater, Orchestra Hall, Marshall Field's, and Buckingham Fountain.

At the hotel's Kitty O'Shea's Pub, the staff speaks and sings with thick Irish brogues as they serve shepherd's pie and hearty lamb stew. Chefs, bartenders, and waitstaff are Irish natives working in the United States on a culinary hotel exchange program with the Irish government. So order a Guinness on tap or an Irish coffee and enjoy the folk music and Irish sing-alongs.

The Hilton Vacation Station offers services, gifts, and information aimed at helping families have fun together. Board games are available, as well as Lincoln logs, Tinkertoys, and that all-time favorite, Mr. Potatohead. The hotel's restaurants have children's menus, and parents receive a family fun kit full of information on nearby city attractions.

Rooms are comfortable and restful. Suite 2412, for example, has pretty east and north views of Grant Park set against Lake Michigan. Natural daylight streams in through windows in the elegant, Italian-marble bathroom.

Chicago Hilton and Towers also has a state-of-the-art athletic club (listing follows).

Michigan Avenue

Chicago Hilton and Towers, 720 S. Michigan Ave., Chicago, IL 60605; (312) 922-4400. 1,543 rooms and suites. Rates average $150-$175.

23 / Non-membership Athletic Club with Pool, Sauna, Weight Room

Chicago Hilton and Towers Athletic Club

Even if you're not a guest at the Chicago Hilton and Towers, you can work out in its ultramodern athletic club. Swim out cramped muscles in a 20-yard heated indoor pool, relax in whirlpool spas and saunas, or jog the cushioned 1/18-mile indoor, banked track. Aerobics classes, massage, tanning beds, and a rooftop sun deck add more choices.

Workout equipment includes Nautilus and Hammer strength weight-training stations, free weights, stair climbers, computerized electronic treadmills, rowing machines, computerized exercise bikes, cross-country ski machines, and other state-of-the-art machines.

"We provide personal training at no extra cost," says club Director Amy Nelson. "Guests can work on their cardiovascular fitness, strength training—even problems like high blood pressure. We also give out complimentary literature on nutrition, weight loss, and many other health and fitness topics."

So don't give up your fitness routine while touring Chicago. Pick up a day pass; you'll feel better in no time.

Michigan Avenue

Chicago Hilton and Towers Athletic Club, 720 S. Michigan Ave., Chicago, IL 60605; (312) 294-6800. Fee for nonhotel guests is $10 for the day. Massages are $30 for a half hour and $50 for an hour.

24 / Admire Chicago's Skyline from the World's Tallest Office Building

Sears Tower

At 110 stories, the Sears Tower is still the world's tallest building. It's hard to believe the Sears empire was the 1886 brainchild of Richard Sears, who sold watches by mail while working as a station agent in North Redwood, Minnesota. Sears and his partner, Alvah Roebuck, opened their first retail store in 1925, in a 12-story building on Chicago's west side. In 1973, the current Sears Tower made its debut at a cost of over $150 million.

Multilingual brochures welcome the 1.3 million tourists who visit Sears Tower each year. A multimedia show, a showcase of Chicago's architectural highlights, and an exhibit about the Tower itself entertain visitors waiting for elevators to the Skydeck.

"One of my favorite experiences," recalls elevator guard John Bednarz, "was the couple who arrived in a wedding gown and tux, ready to get married up top. Their minister went up with them, and the whole ceremony took five minutes. When they came back down, I congratulated them as man and wife."

The 1,600-feet-per-minute ride takes an ear-popping 70 seconds, rocketing you to four-state views and 30-mile visibility. The south view reveals Chicago's industrial sprawl of expressways, railway tracks, and the Chicago River. The west view shows the University of Illinois campus, Northwestern Railroad, and expressways. Gray-green Lake Michigan stars on the east view, decorated with white sailboats and green Grant Park. Most spectacular is the north view in which Chicago's architectural treasures look like toys against the sky.

By the way, Skydeck weddings can't be scheduled in advance. But if you happen to be in an "I do" mood, buy your intended a ticket and enjoy the view.

Michigan Avenue/South Loop

Sears Tower, 233 S. Wacker Dr., Chicago, IL 60606; (312) 875-9696. Hours: October-February 9 a.m.-10 p.m., March-September 9 a.m.-11 p.m. Admission: $4.75-$6.50.

25 / Historic Department Store Overflowing with Luxurious Goods

Marshall Field's

Marshall Field's on State Street is more like a museum of commerce than a store, a virtual "kingdom of thingdom." Magnetic miles of luxurious goods bring to mind all the "desperately needed" things you don't already own. Start out your Field's shopping frenzy near the atrium escalators on the fourth or fifth floors. Admire the iridescent blue and gold mosaic dome designed by Louis Comfort Tiffany in 1907. The 1,600,000 pieces of Favrile glass were laid by hand by 50 artisans who took two years to complete this crown jewel.

Eleven floors at Field's mean it may take a few years to get through the whole store. The lower level, called Marketplace, is where you'll find kitchenware, books, stationery, gourmet foods, candy, wine, flowers, electronics, luggage, and a terrific food court. The first floor has a Gallery of Shops featuring Hermes, Louis Vuitton, Coach, and the famous Frango Mint outpost. From here on up, if you can't find it at Marshall Field's, it may not exist! Look for sportswear for the whole family, furs, bridal gowns, jewelry, swimwear, shoes, suits, dresses, home decor, furniture, and designers from Geoffrey Beene to Yves St. Laurent. For a free style consultation, stop into P.S. Field's on the third floor. For a relaxing lunch or snack, Field's has a variety of restaurants from fish and chips to Mexican, Italian, Chinese, or simply American. The elegant Walnut Room soothes with live classical piano music.

Don't try buying everything in the store on your first visit. You can always come back.

Michigan Avenue/Loop

Marshall Field's, 111 N. State St., Chicago, IL 60202; (312) 781-1000. Monday-Friday 9:45 a.m.-7 p.m., Saturday 9:45 a.m.-6:00 p.m., Sunday noon-5 p.m., monthly Super Sundays, 10 a.m.-5 p.m.

26 / A City Bus Tour with Colorful Anecdotes and Quotes

American Sightseeing

You haven't seen Chicago until you've seen the city through the eyes of American Sightseeing's guide Voyer Howell. Aboard a modern motorcoach, Mr. Howell enthuses and entertains with Chicago's facts and anecdotes: the Calder sculpture that Mr. Howell thinks looks like a "wet chicken" and Chicago's most hated building, Traffic Court. He recommends the John Hancock Center observation deck over the Sears Tower because the Hancock has more attractions close by. (We think you will enjoy both!) Mr. Howell also knows the shopping hours of Michigan Avenue stores such as Tiffany's and Nieman Marcus and likes to joke, "Use my name, you'll get a terrific discount."

You'll be squired in comfort around Chicago in buses with overhead lights, air conditioning, and comfy reclining seats. The North Side tour features the Wrigley Building, the John Hancock Center, Wrigley Field, and a "hug-the-tropical-trees" stop at Lincoln Park Conservatory. Many other tours are available.

All in all, an American Sightseeing tour is a relaxing, stress-free way to get the big picture from a knowledgeable guide who loves his town.

Michigan Avenue/Loop

American Sightseeing, 27 E. Monroe St., Suite 515, Chicago, IL 60603; (312) 427-3100. The company has a variety of general-interest tours, including architecture highlights and Chinatown. Average cost: $15.

27 / Learn Chicago History and Architecture from Expert Guides

Chicago Architecture Foundation

Daniel Burnham, creator of the celebrated Chicago Plan of 1909, would surely be pleased that Chicago has become a living museum of architecture. After all, Chicago gave the world its first skyscraper, developed the iron skeleton and the floating foundation, created the Prairie style of design, and became home to the tallest office building on Earth.

A delightful way to learn about both historic landmark buildings and contemporary structures is to take one of the 50 walking and bus tours conducted by the knowledgeable guides at the Chicago Architecture Foundation. The Loop walking tours consist of "Early Skyscrapers" and "Modern and Beyond."

"Early Skyscrapers" unveils the historic beginnings of the Chicago School of Architecture, focusing on skyscrapers built between 1880 and 1940. You'll visit the art deco Chicago Board of Trade, Louis Sullivan's Auditorium Building, and The Rookery, a national historic landmark.

"Modern and Beyond" explores the international, modern, and post-modern movements, focusing on post-World War II development and the impact of technological changes. You'll learn about the influential Mies van der Rohe and visit the Inland Steel Building and the James R. Thompson Center.

Farther afield, a 30-mile bus tour showcases Chicago's diversity, wending through the Loop, Hyde Park, the Gold Coast, historic districts, university campuses, and stopping to tour Frank Lloyd Wright's Robie House. Other tours visit Chicago's Historic House Museums, the 1836 Clarke House and the 1887 Glessner House. Cruises down the Chicago River spotlight 53 significant architectural sights.

Michigan Avenue

Chicago Architecture Foundation, 224 S. Michigan Ave., Chicago, IL 60604-2507; (312) 922-3432. Recorded tour information: 922-TOUR. Cost: $8-$25.

28 / Library Featuring Story Hours, Language Labs, Music Rooms, Author Readings

Harold Washington Library

A portrait of Bambi hangs next to a grinning stuffed Humpty Dumpty. Miniature bears wearing red bow ties sip party punch inside the Doll House. Purple macaws fly on green kites suspended over acres of reading tables, a shark jaw exhibit, and seashells from beaches around the world. A Paul Bunyan poster says "Books tell tall tales—Read."

It's story hour at the Thomas Hughes Children's Library. Sitting quietly on gray-carpeted steps in an alcove festive with winged elephants and creatures with tails, wide-eyed children listen intently as the librarian reads aloud.

Anyone exhausted from city sightseeing will enjoy a peaceful afternoon at Chicago's new library, one of the largest municipal public circulating libraries in the United States. Ten floors of books indexed on computer, a foreign language lab, a music listening center, a Chicago authors room, and a gift and coffee shop present a multitude of rejuvenating choices for the whole family. An elegant two-story Winter Garden on the ninth floor shows off Chicago's Loop skyline.

The children's library on the second floor has over 100,000 picture books, easy readers, classics, science projects, reference materials, and magazines. Storytime "extravaganzas" happen regularly every week, as well as children's films, games, songs, puppetry workshops, and plays.

Treat yourself and the kids to some quiet time in a relaxing setting that's educational and free.

South Loop

The Chicago Public Library, Harold Washington Library Center, 400 S. State St., Chicago, IL 60605; (312) 747-4200. Hours: Monday 9 a.m.-7 p.m., Tuesday, Thursday 11 a.m.-7 p.m., Wednesday, Friday, Saturday 9 a.m.-5 p.m., Sunday 1 p.m.-5 p.m.

29 / Chicago's Grammy Award-winning World-Class Symphony

Chicago Symphony Orchestra

Chicagoans boast about the Chicago Symphony Orchestra (CSO), and rightfully so: few orchestras have won 52 Grammy Awards from the National Academy of Recording Arts and Sciences.

The *Wall Street Journal* heralds the Chicago Symphony Orchestra as "alluring and accomplished"; the *Miami Herald* notes that the CSO "remains one of the world's supreme ensembles." *The New York Times* enthuses, "On page after page of the score, the sheer orchestral virtuosity took one's breath away." Performances are greeted with unbridled enthusiasm abroad and at home; in 1994, 235,000 seats were sold *before* opening night in Chicago.

During the current season, the CSO will tour Japan and record Tchaikovsky, Berlioz, Bruckner, Shostakovich, and Bartok. A dazzling number of star conductors will be welcomed, including Sir Georg Solti, Pierre Boulez, Zubin Mehta, James De Preist, and Leonard Slatkin. CSO radio broadcasts will be heard over more than 400 stations nationwide, including WFMT in Chicago.

The symphony's whirlwind of activities and accomplishments occur under the masterful guidance of Music Director Daniel Barenboim, who became the ninth music director of the CSO in 1991. In his role at the CSO, Barenboim conducts many performances in Chicago and abroad, commissions major contemporary works, trains young orchestral players and conductors, and earns accolades from critics. "Mr. Barenboim is a giant musician . . . keeping Chicago on the musical map, as the orchestral capital of the United States."

Michigan Avenue

Chicago Symphony Orchestra, 220 S. Michigan Ave., Chicago, IL 60604; (312) 435-6666. For tickets, phone Monday-Saturday 10 a.m.-6 p.m., Sunday noon-4 p.m.

30 / Landmark Fine Arts Museum Spanning Forty Centuries of Human Creativity

Art Institute of Chicago

"Any day you visit the Art Institute, your spirits are uplifted by all the magnificent things to see," says Ruth Powell, an Art Institute docent. "Especially on a gray winter day, the brilliant colors, shapes, and forms will transform you."

Ruth Powell should know. She's been leading tours of the Art Institute for school children every week for thirty-plus years. "Whether the kids are from an inner-city school or a private school," she says, "my job is to get them to talk, think, and get excited about art."

The museum's Kraft General Foods Education Center is designed especially for children and their families, offering special exhibits, artist demonstrations, hands-on workshops, and story-telling hours. One special exhibit features a cross section of masterpieces from the museum, with interactive learning activities and computer games.

One of the world's leading museums, the Institute's collection spans forty centuries of human creativity. From Rembrandt paintings to African wood carvings, displays include a dazzling variety of art—sculpture, prints, drawings, photographs, textiles, architectural models, miniatures, and, of course, paintings.

Ruth Powell notes that the Museum's Arms and Armor collections are most popular with kids, as are the Impressionist paintings of Monet and Renoir. "The Art Institute is my home away from home," she enthuses. "If I could, I'd wake up there every morning." *Michigan Avenue*

Art Institute of Chicago, 111 S. Michigan Ave., Chicago, IL 60603; (312) 443-3600. Hours: Monday, Wednesday, Thursday, Friday 10:30 a.m.-4:30 p.m., Tuesday 10:30 a.m.-8 p.m., Saturday 10 a.m.-5 p.m., Sunday and holidays noon-5 p.m. Admission: $3.25-$6.50. Collection highlight tours: 2 p.m. daily. Lectures by the staff and visiting scholars: Tuesdays at 12:15 and 6 p.m.

31 / Theater Presenting Classics, Revivals, Musicals, New Works

Goodman Theatre

"Chicago is a rich rich theater city," notes Goodman's Associate Artistic Director Michael Maggio, "and we offer theatergoers an artistic mix of classical revivals, musicals, and new works."

The Goodman Theatre, Chicago's oldest and largest residential theater, was the 1992 recipient of the Special Tony Award for Outstanding Regional Theatre. Notable recent productions include Artistic Director Robert Falls's stagings of *The Night of the Iguana* and *The Iceman Cometh*; Associate Director Frank Galati's world premiere *She Always Said, Pablo* and *The Good Person of Setzuan*; Michael Maggio's *Sunday in the Park with George* and his world-premiere stagings of *Wings* and *Black Snow*; *Death and the King's Horseman* by Nobel Laureate Wole Soyinka; and August Wilson's Pulitzer Prize-winning plays *The Piano Lesson* and *Fences*.

Goodman has staged new works by Edward Albee, Samuel Beckett, John Guare, Emily Mann, Scott McPherson, Steve Tesich, and Tennessee Williams. During the holidays residents and tourists enjoy the Goodman's annual *A Christmas Carol*; and throughout the year productions by the Stratford Shakespearean Festival of Canada, the American Repertory Theatre, and the Negro Ensemble Company.

Maggio says, "Our location on the lakefront next to the Art Institute, across from the Grant Park Concert Stage, is a great part of the Chicago experience. We're proud to be right in the center of a thriving entertainment scene."

Michigan Avenue

Goodman Theatre, 200 S. Columbus Dr., Chicago, IL 60603-6491; (312) 443-3800.

32 / Center for Free Films, Music, Dance, and Visitor Information

Chicago Cultural Center

Back when the Cultural Center was the Chicago Public Library, I never got any work done there. I would go with a briefcase of papers, but then end up distracted and astonished by the splendid Tiffany dome in Preston Bradley Hall, with its Zodiac symbols and mosaic scrolls. Then I'd wander into the GAR Rotunda to admire the pink marble walls with backlit windows of translucent glass blocks. I'd float down the grand staircase, pretending to be Audrey Hepburn or Grace Kelly in a drop-dead beaded gown. Multicolored mosaics, bronze sconces, soaring arches, and inscribed quotes from the world's greatest writers—who could get anything done amidst all this magnificence?

Fortunately, the Harold Washington Library at 400 South State Street now houses the books and collections. But here at the Cultural Center there's more than ever going on: The Chicago Office of Tourism operates the city's Visitor Information Center, handing out free literature, maps, and schedules of the Cultural Center's free concerts and movies. The Welcome Center presents a short city orientation video, as well as exhibits of historic photos, posters, and enlarged street maps. Hedwig Dance rehearses and performs here, and the new Studio Theater stages readings, poetry, and lectures. Michigan Avenue galleries showcase the work of local and emerging artists, and the Landmark Chicago gallery displays photos and architectural artifacts. The Museum of Broadcast Communications features radio and TV exhibits, a working studio, and a delightful gift shop.

On Saturdays, a Loop tour train guide shares insights on the history and architecture of Chicago from the CTA elevated train. Tickets are available at the Cultural Center.

Michigan Avenue/North Loop

Chicago Cultural Center, 78 E. Washington St., Chicago, IL 60602; (312) 744-2400. Hours: Monday-Saturday 10 a.m.-5 p.m.

33 / City Garden Oasis Soothes Frazzled Nerves

Amoco Building Plaza Garden and Fountain

Time to escape Chicago's din. Walk south on Michigan Avenue to Randolph Street and east to the Amoco Building, a square, white 1,136-foot tower, seventh tallest in the world.

An oasis of trees and flowers soothes jangled nerves. Shimmering water splashes a symphony for weary ears. Severe city rectangles are softened to curves and sprays of water arc into a circular fountain surrounded by granite benches that beckon to tired feet. A white-iron Juliet balcony takes the high view over gardens of dwarf fountain grass, grapeleaf anemone, and wartburg star asters. Monarch butterflies flit among yellow black-eyed susans, fat bees nuzzle into golden daylilies, and crickets add their chirps to the musical fanfare.

Nestled among the trees are gazebos with glass-umbrella roofs that look like white mushroom caps and act as protective sunscreens. Executives with briefcases, mothers with toddlers, and tourists with shopping bags all take a break, enjoying a glittering, watery world that drowns out the city's screeching buses and honking cars.

Relax, refresh.

Michigan Avenue/North Loop

Amoco Building Plaza Garden and Fountain, 200 E. Randolph St., Chicago, IL 60601.

34 / Italian Breakfast Alfresco, Lunch and Dinner Indoors

Nick and Tony's

One of the great pleasures of Chicago is dining alfresco, taking in splendid city views. Enjoy a sunrise breakfast along the banks of the Chicago River from Nick and Tony's art deco patio, decorated with Italian marble and colorful flower gardens.

Start your day with a fresh baked pumpkin, cranberry, or chocolate oreo muffin; an orange or chocolate chip mint scone; an onion, blueberry, or sesame bagel; almond or chocolate hazelnut biscotti; or granola with fresh fruit. Get your caffeine fix from a cappuccino, latte, or iced mocha, or energize with freshly squeezed orange juice.

If 6 a.m. is too early for you, then come back for a homestyle Italian lunch or dinner. This newly opened 1940s-style restaurant features dining rooms decorated with vintage Italian posters and lovely Venetian murals. A 40-foot bar undulates through the elegant dining room, with alabaster and bronze chandeliers and mahogany and walnut parquet floors. An open kitchen provides a great view of Chef David Del Gatto at work.

Some of Chef Del Gatto's signature dishes include Osso Bucco; grilled Swordfish Pizzaiola; and Sicilian Meatball Ragu with peas, artichokes, and mashed potatoes. Antipasti include Italian Wedding Soup; prosciutto with roasted onions, red peppers and Parmesan; and baked stuffed eggplant. Other favorites include porcini risotto and delicious thin-crust pizzas. A variety of American and Italian wines is offered, many from small wineries and many by the glass.

Begin your Chicago sightseeing day outdoors, or end a perfect day indoors in one of Chicago's newest and friendliest Italian eateries.

The Loop

Nick and Tony's, One E. Wacker Drive, Chicago, IL 60601; (312) 467-9449. Hours: 6 a.m.-11 p.m. daily, valet parking after 5 p.m. Major credit cards accepted.

35 / Elegant Hotel Hosting International Visitors

Fairmont Hotel Chicago

The lobby is grand, with creamy marble columns, celadon urns filled with crimson bromeliads, and a sleek baby grand in the bar. Tourists, shoppers, and business executives mill about conversing in French, Spanish, Japanese, and German, as well as in English. Located in Illinois Center overlooking Lake Michigan, the Chicago Yacht Harbor, and Grant Park, this elegant 692-room hotel is perfectly located for exploring downtown Chicago on foot.

Rooms are extra spacious with writing desks, multiline phones, and electric shoe polishers. Marble bathrooms have oversized tubs, separate shower stalls, radio, and TV for CNN junkies.

The Fairmont's Primavera Ristorante and Bar features fresh pasta, seafood, veal, chicken, and gourmet pizza. The Primavera Singers entertain guests at dinner with favorite songs from opera, operetta, and musical comedy. One romantic couple celebrated their fiftieth anniversary by having the singers perform songs from their wedding.

Dining at Entre Nous, a soothing, serene restaurant with crystal chandeliers, velvety mushroom chairs, and jungle palms, guarantees a relaxing evening. Enjoy crab cakes with lobster sauce, fresh salmon with asparagus, and a divine lemon meringue pie, accompanied by a glass or bottle of 1988 Groth Cabernet Sauvignon. The fine wine collection is extensive.

Music at the Fairmont's Metropole night club is eclectic and electric. Spend the next day working out at the adjacent Athletic Club Illinois Center or playing golf at the nearby public city course (also featured in this guide).

Michigan Avenue/North Loop

Fairmont Hotel Chicago, 200 N. Columbus Dr., Chicago, IL 60601; (312) 565-8000. Central Reservations: (800) 527-4727. Rates: $179 (city view)-$269 (lake view), weekends $109-$119.

36 / Swank Hotel Nightclub Presenting Jazz, Pop, Blues

Metropole

Swank is in again: round marble tables lit by soft candlelight, leather chairs to sink into, waiters resplendent in formal tuxedos. Illinois artist Ed Hinkley's murals add to the stylish, sophisticated ambience at Metropole.

Attention centers on the tiny stage lit in red and blue spots, where guest artists groove to their own tunes, accompanied by piano, bass, drums, and sax.

Live musical entertainment is diverse, varying from jazz to pop to blues. Recent artists included pop/jazz artist Bobby Caldwell; pianist Alex Bugnon; vocal stylist Kenny Rankin; acoustic guitarist Craig Chaquico; Brazilian artists Astrud Gilberto and Laurindo Almeida; saxophonists Mark Johnson and Stanley Turrentine; and Chicago's own Shadowfax.

Junior Walker and the All Stars were a recent blast from the past, performing their greatest hits including "Pucker Up Buttercup," "These Eyes," and "Come See about Me." Vocalist Jimmy Scott, lead singer for Lionel Hampton's band in 1948, got rave reviews with his forever-wonderful hits "The Masquerade Is Over," "Imagination," and "Oh What I Wouldn't Give."

The schedule of artists changes every week, so call or drop by to see who's performing. A dinner jazz package is available Wednesday through Friday evenings in the Fairmont Hotel's Entre Nous and Primavera Restaurants. For $39, guests enjoy a three-course dinner and a ticket to a Metropole show.

Swank is in again, so wear something glamorous.

Michigan Avenue/North Loop

Metropole, at the Fairmont Hotel, 200 N. Columbus Dr., Chicago, IL 60601. Tickets: through the hotel at (312) 565-6665 or Ticketmaster, (312) 559-1212.

37 / Six-Level Health Club for Serious Workouts and Pampering

Athletic Club Illinois Center

Grown men cling like Spiderman to a seven-story climbing wall. Executives in top shape tear around the running track at breakneck speed. Fast trackers put in their miles swimming laps in the 25-yard competition pool.

Working out is serious business at the Athletic Club Illinois Center. Certified instructors help guests work on stress reduction, weight loss, body sculpting, and cardiovascular conditioning. Aerobics classes are held hourly: high impact, low impact, step, conditioning, and aqua aerobics. Still energetic? Pick up a game of basketball, volleyball, racquetball, or squash.

If relaxation and rejuvenation are your idea of working out, check into the Athletic Club's New Heights Spa. Massage therapy includes Swedish, reflexology, shiatsu, aromatherapy, and Moor Therapy back treatments. Body treatments include loofa scrubs, turkish salt glows, aloe-herbal wraps, contouring body masks, and Hungarian Kur baths. Finish off a day of pampering with a facial, manicure, and pedicure.

Contact your hotel to see about getting a pass to the club.

Just a few blocks from the Athletic Club is Illinois Center Golf, a nine-hole public par-three course and natural-grass practice range. Sign up for private lessons or a clinic for advanced players, beginners, business execs, or women only. The Lake Michigan water hazard is challenging, but it's the perfect urban course for a busy golfer who has just enough time for a lunchhour round. Try not to hit any skyscraper windows.

The Loop

Athletic Club Illinois Center, 211 N. Stetson Ave., Chicago, IL 60601; (312) 616-9000. Hours: Monday-Friday 6 a.m.-10 p.m., Saturday-Sunday 8 a.m.-8 p.m. Fees: $12-$18 per day. Illinois Center Golf, 221 N. Columbus Dr., Chicago, IL 60601; (312) 616-1234. Open to the public.

38 / Authentic Chicago Jazz in a Casual Neighborhood Bar & Restaurant

Andy's Jazz Club

How many jazz clubs have their own song, penned by a professional musician? Framed in all its glory on Andy's wall of fame is this appreciative tune by Chicago's renowned jazz artist Johnny Frigo:

From five, til eight each week night
The way to sate your appetite
Is to dig that jazz that's out of sight, at Andy's.

Forget New York, forget L.A.,
I'm here to say there ain't no way,
They're gonna cut the jazz that they play, down at Andy's.

What could be more relaxing after a real hard day,
Than to have a brew or two while listening to
Music that has something to say?
So meet your date, and celebrate on Hubbard Street
Just east of State
And don't be late
Cuz the jazz is great at Andy's.*

We couldn't agree more. Call for the daily smorgasbord of solo, duo, trio, quartet, quintet, swing, and bop till you drop.

Sandwiches, soup, and salads are served at lunchtime; pasta, prime rib, and homemade pizza are dinner choices. Swing by.

Michigan Avenue/North

Andy's Jazz Club, 11 E. Hubbard St., Chicago, IL 60611; (312) 642-6805. Lunch and conversational jazz, weekdays noon-2:30 p.m.; jazz at 5 and 9 p.m.; Saturday, early bird sets 6:30 p.m.-9 p.m. Kitchen open until midnight.

*Lyrics reprinted by permission of Johnny Frigo, ASCAP.

39 / Chicago's Heralded Oyster and Seafood Palace

Shaw's Crab House

A five-foot-long silvery blue swordfish arches over the bar. A green neon sign proclaims "softshell crabs are now in season." Even the table lamp is oceanic: a nubile mermaid poses coquettishly on a seashell.

Shaw's menu lists oysters not only by name but also by geography. Would you care for fresh oysters from California, Oregon, or Virginia? How about Massachusetts or Maine? Perhaps you're feeling international tonight, so order the oysters flown in this morning from Chile or New Zealand. Enjoy them on the half shell, Rockefeller, or pan fried, with a dry, crisp glass of "clean finishing" wine. Shaw's is Chicago's veritable oyster palace, with platters heaped with oysters and an oyster festival in October.

What, you don't want oysters?

So settle for Brazilian twin lobster tails, sautéed sea scallops, or Alaskan King Crab legs. Texas stone crab, pan-fried yellow lake perch, grilled garlic shrimp, or planked Lake Superior whitefish. Vegetarians relish the seasonal vegetable platter, Caesar salad, black bean soup, and fresh corn on the cob from Tom's Farm in Huntley, Illinois. Seasonal specials might be Virginia softshell crabs, cashew-crusted Mississippi catfish, grilled Florida red grouper, or char-glazed Hawaiian opah.

Next door to the dining room is the Blue Crab Lounge Oyster Bar, where oyster friends await you on ice. How about the sampler plate of malpeque, chiloe, Long Island Sound, coromandel, or rilan oysters?

You don't know where they're from?

Stop by, and bring a map.

Michigan Avenue/North

Shaw's Crab House, 21 E. Hubbard St., Chicago, IL 60611; (312) 527-2722. Lunch: Monday-Friday 11:30 a.m.-2 p.m., dinner: Monday-Friday 5:30-10 p.m., Friday-Saturday 11:30 a.m.-11 p.m., Sunday 5-10 p.m. Entrées: $12.95-$18.95. Reservations suggested.

40 / Antiques & Collectibles from Thailand, Myanmar, Laos

The Golden Triangle

Leave Chicago's hubbub and journey to the mountains and rainforests and visit the hill peoples of the Golden Triangle: Thailand, Myanmar, and Laos. From a world where craftsmanship is prized, owners Douglas Van Tress and Chauwarin Tuntisak have uncovered a fascinating array of Southeast Asian artifacts and antiques.

On one wall a handcarved, winged dragon flies over undulating mountains in a sea of teak clouds. Perhaps he is a Naga water dragon, mythical protector of temples, palaces, and royalty.

A rose-and-lime-colored Burmese ceiling panel shows lotus flowers unfolding among an orchestra of smiling musicians. What are the mysteries behind their smiles?

The Golden Triangle's success stems from the co-owners's hard-earned Rolodex of Asian contacts, especially from Thailand where Tuntisak has family. Tuntisak's sister Jiriporn sent a crate of Thai wood carvings back in 1988, launching their first store. Demand was so great that the duo was able to move to this larger Hubbard Street location during the summer of 1993.

Several times a year, Mr. Tuntisak explores Thai villages for antiques and crafts. He also buys goods from Laos and Cambodia at the Thai border.

Both Van Tress and Tuntisak seem to cherish each of their Golden Triangle treasures, from teakwood water buffalo, to a 6-foot-long log carved into a rainforest of elephants, to a stately Thai teak spirit house. But anything from The Golden Triangle can be yours, if you and your credit cards are worthy.

Michigan Avenue/North

The Golden Triangle, 72 W. Hubbard St., Chicago, IL 60610; (312) 755-1266. Hours: Monday-Friday 10 a.m.-7 p.m., Saturday 10 a.m.-6 p.m., closed Sunday. Prices range from $4 to $7,500, with most items in the $100-$300 range.

41 / Where Chicago's Deep-Dish Pizza Was Born

Pizzeria Uno / Pizzeria Due

An elegant gray and green Victorian mansion in the midst of urban madness is an unlikely setting for a pizza parlor. Kawasakis and Harleys roar by and horse-drawn carriages clip-clop amid four lanes of speeding traffic. The stately Medinah Temple stands guard across the street. People stand in a line that snakes around the block.

Back in 1943, a bar owner named Ike Sewell wondered if people would be interested in a new dish: flaky crust lining a deep pan, loaded with mozzarella cheese, layered with sausage and fresh tomatoes. Not only were they interested, they were obsessed. Mr. Sewell became king of Chicago's deep-dish pizza, celebrated worldwide. Two tons of pizza sauce, 8,000 pounds of mozzarella, and a truckload of Italian plum tomatoes are delivered each week to keep up with the demand. Mr. Sewell's original restaurant, Pizzeria Uno, and his second restaurant, Pizzeria Due, are always mobbed. People can't seem to get enough of this stuff.

Once an order is placed, it may take an hour before the fragrant pizza shows up at your table. But the wait is worth it: people chew contentedly like cows, smiling and nodding to each other. After two gigantic slices, their eyes bulge, they look down at rounded bellies and say those magic words, "Wrap it to go, please."

Outside another crop of hopefuls waits its turn, dreaming of deep-dish pizza heaven.

Michigan Avenue/North

Pizzeria Uno, 29 E. Ohio St., Chicago, IL 60611; (312) 321-1000. Hours: Monday-Friday 11:30-1 a.m., Saturday 11:30-2 a.m., Sunday 11:30 a.m.-11:30 p.m. No reservations.

Pizzeria Due, 619 N. Wabash Ave., Chicago, IL 60611; (312) 943-2400. Hours: Monday-Thursday 11:30-1:30 a.m., Friday-Saturday 11:30-2:30 a.m., Sunday 11:30 a.m.-11:30 p.m. No reservations.

42 / Over Fifty Fantastic Boutiques along the Chicago River

North Pier Festival Market

Along the cool green Chicago River, the air is fresh and the sky-line views breathtaking. Fifty shops overflow with temptations at this commercial pier turned mall.

Beautiful shearling coats at Overland Outfitters will keep you cozy in winter; colorful kites at The Kite Harbor will keep you company in summer. Boutiques cater to hot chili lovers, rainforest savers, and major sports fans. Splurge on a nautical painting or a dolphin sculpture at Call of the Sea. Take home a logo-emblazoned T-shirt or coffee mug from City of Chicago. Light Wave offers unique 3-D holograms to hang on your wall or wear on your wrist. Amigos & Us is a worldly bazaar of handmade clothing, and Deceptions boasts fabulous fake jewels.

Riverside dining is fun at Marley's Floating Calypso Hut or Dick's Dock, where the table decor is a Corona six-pack. Gorge on succulent crab legs at Old Carolina Crab House, or feast from North Pier's fast-food buffet. After lunch, there's more to do: explore The Bicycle Museum, play a round at City Golf, or peer into a cyberspace future at Virtual Reality. Rent a bike for an hour or a day from Turin Bikes, and see the lakefront up close. For warm-blooded sports types, Berry Scuba will outfit you with diving gear and guides if you're certified. Learn about Chicago's history and architecture on a "Chicago from the Lake" boat tour.

Or just relax near the cascading waterfalls of Centennial Fountain a block south, where you can watch the busy world go by.

Michigan Avenue/North

North Pier Festival Market, 435 E. Illinois St., Chicago, IL 60611; (312) 836-4300. Monday-Thursday 10 a.m.-9 p.m., Friday-Saturday 10 a.m.-10 p.m., Sunday 11 a.m.-7 p.m.

43 / Enjoy Chicago's Skyline from Lake Michigan aboard a Yacht

Chicago from the Lake

Lake Michigan rolls deep green, the sun blazes yellow, and a cool breeze carries our guide's history lesson. No textbooks, no uncomfortable classroom chairs. Just the gentle motion of *The Marquette*, a beautiful, blue-and-white ship carrying us past elegant white corporate monoliths, shiny black high-rises, and sleek green condominiums. It's hard to believe that all this was wilderness to explorers Father Marquette and Louis Jolliet back in 1673, or that a great city was destroyed in the Chicago Fire of 1871, or that Chicago was a rebuilt miracle by the time of the 1933 Chicago World's Fair.

Our guide points out the domed Adler Planetarium, the Shedd Aquarium, and the Roman columns of the Museum of Natural History. Hundreds of gleaming yachts bob in the harbor as Buckingham Fountain splashes skyward nearby.

Sea gulls dive for their lunch as passengers snack on fresh blueberry muffins, lemonade, and coffee. Teens decked out in Bulls and Bears outfits ogle towering walls of glass and concrete along the Chicago River, awed by the challenges to, and success stories of, the architects who created them.

Back at the dock ninety minutes later, our guide bids us farewell with Daniel Burnham's 1900s action call: "Make no little plans, they have no magic to stir men's souls...."

Michigan Avenue/Lake Shore Drive

Chicago from the Lake, 455 E. Illinois St., Chicago, IL 60611; (312) 527-2002, departing from North Pier, at the corner of Illinois St. and McClurg Ct., ninety-minute lake and/or river cruises, architectural and/or historical. Seven days a week, 9 a.m.-4 p.m. Cost: Adults $16, Seniors, AAA $14, kids ages 9-18 $11, kids 8 and younger are free.

44 / Renovated Pier Featuring Theaters, Restaurants, Shops, Ferris Wheel

Navy Pier

A Chicago landmark since 1916, Navy Pier served as a military training facility during two world wars and as a university campus, but fell into disuse during the 1970s and 1980s while the city debated its future.

Navy Pier is now very much alive and well. As of the summer of 1994, visitors and locals have been enjoying Skyline Stage, a 1,500-seat open-air theater with a vaulted roof and, as the name suggests, excellent city skyline views. Performers range from rock bands to gospel groups, comedians to international theater troupes.

By the summer of 1995, the Pier's Family Pavilion will house Chicago Children's Museum, an IMAX theater, and a variety of restaurants and shops. Beyond the Pavilion, you can explore Crystal Gardens—a 32,000-square-foot indoor botanical park—glide around an ice skating rink, or join your kids for an unforgettable view of Chicago from a 150-foot Ferris wheel.

Special events are regularly scheduled and include poetry festivals, fishing days, navy ship tours, and, on July 3, Chicago's annual firework display on the lake, which seems more spectacular every year.

From the south dock several luxury yachts offer brunch, lunch, dinner, and midnight cruises. Take the free trolley buses, bike, jog, or just amble along enjoying the view of Lake Michigan.

Michigan Avenue/North

Navy Pier, 600 E. Grand Ave., Chicago, IL 60611; (312) 791-PIER. Parking and public transportation are close by; accessible for visitors with disabilities.

45 / Museum for Children on Recycling, Relationships, Computers, Creativity

Chicago Children's Museum

Meet Fadouma Omar who arrived in Chicago in 1993 from eastern Africa, Paz Calle from El Salvador, or Lang and Sith from Laos. They're part of the "Grandparents" photo exhibit at Chicago Children's Museum, through which kids learn cultural identity from family stories. The museum encourages kids to bring their own abuelita or ojiisan for a photo session.

Chicago Children's Museum believes that children learn best by expressing creativity, developing self-esteem, and solving problems in a safe, playful environment of interactive exhibits.

Kids learn "The Stinking Truth about Garbage" in a humorous, innovative exhibit. Children also learn ways their families can recycle paper, metals, foods, and plastics. Teenage volunteers teach young Picassos and O'Keeffes how to create art from discarded toys, such as a life-sized horse made from recycled sunglasses, broken dolls, and bits of shoes.

From the "Buildings and Lego" exhibit, visitors learn about world-famous architecture; "Magic and Masquerades" highlights West Africa's cultural traditions; "Newsbrief" puts kids on late-breaking TV news; a difficult wheelchair course helps children appreciate the navigation problems of the physically challenged.

Children are encouraged to take a break from computers and take up the "lost art" of letter writing. There's even a mailbox stuffed with letters where new pen pals wait to find each other.

Michigan Avenue

Chicago Children's Museum, Navy Pier, 600 E. Grand Ave., Chicago, IL 60611; (312) 527-1000. Hours: preschool Tuesday-Friday 10 a.m.-12:30 p.m., general Tuesday-Friday 12:30-4:30 p.m., Saturday, Sunday 10 a.m.-4:30 p.m., Thursday, free day 5-8 p.m. Admission: $2.50-$3.50.

46 / Innovative Italian Cuisine in a Sophisticated Setting

Grappa

Polished wood columns and floors gleam from the light of soft, pumpkin-hued Milanese lamps suspended from the ceiling. Thick strands of garlic bulbs adorning a wrought iron trellis accent a beautiful array of grappa bottles. The wait staff is elegant in taupe silk shirts and black trousers.

Designer Mark Knauer's serene setting is perfect, allowing diners to focus on Chef Dean Zanella's menu: a lighter, contemporary interpretation of classic Italian cuisine.

His appetizer of grilled polpi with black beans, chiles, and marjoram, for example, offers a delightfully fresh combination of flavors, as do the gamberi-grilled shrimp stuffed with scallops, pinenuts, and rosemary.

Entrées are diverse and creative: papardelle with duck, roasted fennel, portobello mushrooms and port sauce; homemade ravioli stuffed with butternut squash, with a walnut cream sauce; grilled tuna with radicchio, lentil puree, and sage olive oil; sautéed veal chops with parmigiano potatoes, wilted greens, and balsamic sauce. Whole red snapper in tomatoes and chile is a spicy surprise.

Salads are anything but ordinary: smoked trout, arugula, and cipolline onions in a fragrant pinenut dressing; or warm radicchio and spinach with buffalo mozzarella in a pancetta dressing.

Deserts are decadent so forget your diet and savor the flourless chocolate cake with pistachio cream sauce.

Created by an all star team featuring Roger Greenfield, Ted Kasemir, and Giovanni Garelli, Grappa is a bright and welcome new star on Chicago's restaurant horizon.

Michigan Avenue

Grappa, 200 E. Chestnut St., Chicago, IL 60611; (312) 337-4500. Hours: Monday-Saturday 11 a.m.-11 p.m. Sunday 4-11 p.m. Bar open until 2 a.m.

47 / Home Decor in a Historic City Mansion

City Source

Located a few blocks west of Chicago's Michigan Avenue shopping mecca is a charming, 100-year-old mansion, now a renovated space of sunny windows and soaring ceilings, home to City Source.

"We specialize in decorative accessories for the home," says co-owner Cyndi LaBarge, "that you won't find in department stores like Neiman Marcus or Marshall Field's." City Source is known for unique photo frames, ceramics, furniture, and unusual collectibles. Photo frames are whimsical yet practical, with colored tiles embedded in stone; delicate, honey-colored bamboo; or gold-painted wood. Violet and topaz crackle-glass vases bring back 1930s memories. Candle holders are swathed in bronze metallic mesh, and swank travel cases are wrapped in vintage fabrics. Hand-designed greeting cards emblazoned with tea cups include real tea bags. Photo albums are covered in elegant fabrics and soft leathers. White ceramic serving platters with gold buttons are designed to add a touch of humor to any dinner table.

Many of City Source's items are signed by the artists, including dramatic decorative plates by Alexis Hernandez, who uses early European and American prints to achieve intriguing trompe l'oeil effects.

City Source originally specialized in needlepoint crafts when the shop first opened in 1983, and the second floor still offers extensive patterns and supplies for needlepoint hobbyists, as well as delightful floral and fruit needlepoint pillows, ready to go home.

Michigan Avenue/North

City Source, 28 E. Huron St., Chicago, IL 60611; (312) 664-5499. Hours: Monday-Friday 11 a.m.-6 p.m., Saturday 10 a.m.-5 p.m.

48 / See Where the *Chicago Tribune* Is Printed, Distributed

Chicago Freedom Center

"Welcome to the *Chicago Tribune*," announces the videotape narrator, "where we capture the drama and emotion that make up the news. Today's events will be tomorrow's headlines."

Visitors touring the Freedom Center begin their tour with an eight-minute-long orientation video on the history of the Pulitzer Prize-winning *Chicago Tribune*, and how the paper's departments work together to create, publish, and distribute some 700,000 papers each day.

At Freedom Center, where the press room and circulation departments are located, you walk past dinosaur-sized blue presses printing 70,000 papers every hour. Giant rolls of newsprint, made from pine, spruce, and poplar trees, are fed into the press, which runs 24 hours a day, 7 days a week, 365 days a year. The warehouse stores 26,000 rolls of newsprint, each weighing 2,000 pounds.

Wearing a navy blue *Chicago Tribune* tie, our guide outlines the many changes he has observed during his 51 years in the pressroom. "You all better learn everything about computers," he instructs two teenage boys, "you can't do a thing without them." Indeed, the presses are computer controlled down to the most minute operation.

The video and walking tour, which takes about an hour-and-a-half, is a fascinating look at how that newspaper on your breakfast table this morning was created.

Michigan Avenue/North

Chicago Freedom Center, 777 W. Chicago Ave., Chicago, IL 60610; (312) 222-2116. Hours: Monday-Friday at 9:30, 10:30, 11:30 a.m., 1, 2, and 3 p.m. Reservations necessary, children should be at least 10. Free admission and parking.

49 / Fresh Made-to-Order Food Court in a Delightful Shopping Mall

Food Life

In his former life, Chef Michael Cech might have been an octopus. In his last job, he cooked for 40,000 people a day at Las Vegas's Luxor Hotel. Now at Chicago's Food Life, he's scaled down a bit, cooking for a mere 6,000 hungry diners seeking healthful food each day.

Banners throughout the cavernous dining rooms proclaim "everyone is unique." People scurry in every direction, mesmerized by the variety of international cuisines cooked to order, served from brightly lit "food stations."

"Everything we serve is made fresh each day," says Chef Cech. "We're giving people new taste sensations, many low fat, to eat here or take home. How many restaurants encourage you to taste a bite of anything before you order?"

Choices are mind boggling: Mongolian barbecue with noodles or brown rice, home smoked ribs and rotisserie chicken, fresh pasta with no-fat marinara sauce, vegetarian pizza on a multigrain crust, cobb and Caesar salads with light dressings, tacos with nonfat black beans and yogurt instead of sour cream, grilled fresh vegetables, espresso, fruit juices without sugar, brownies and cakes, and power drinks with bee pollen.

Leaflets on health and nutrition are free, offering tips including "Ten Steps to a Better Body Image" and "Healthy Advice for Every Day," which suggests you "enjoy quiet time daily for 15 minutes" and "express your emotions."

Food Life is proof that fast food can be healthful and great tasting.

Michigan Avenue

Food Life, 835 N. Michigan Ave., Water Tower Place Mezzanine Level, Chicago, IL 60611; (312) 335-3663. Hours: Monday-Saturday 11 a.m.-10 p.m., juice, espresso, and corner bakery 7:45 a.m.-10 p.m.; Sunday 11 a.m.-9 p.m., juice, espresso and corner bakery 7:45 a.m.-9 p.m.

50 / Discover Four Midwest States from 1,030 Feet Up

The John Hancock Center

"Dad, I don't know if I like this elevator ride," says an 8-year-old boy in a Kansas City T-shirt. "Don't worry, we're only going up 94 floors," laughs his father. Thirty-nine seconds later, elevator doors slide open and the boy bounds out. "Look at the cool view!" he yells.

It's definitely cool at 1,030 feet above North Michigan Avenue, right in the heart of Chicago's "Magnificent Mile." Kind of gives you a new perspective on the word *magnificent*.

To the east, a turquoise Lake Michigan converges with a gray-blue horizon. Chicago's metropolis is a Tinkertoy maze of miniature buildings, cars, and sailboats. The north shows the urban sprawl of offices, brownstones, and the almond slice of Oak Street beach. To the south is a ribbon of the Chicago River, snaking through a tunnel of buildings. The Field Museum, Shedd Aquarium, Alder Planetarium, Skyline Stage, and original Water Tower, now a visitors' center, all come into view.

"One of the best times to come up here is around sunset," suggests security guard Thomas Weathers, Jr. "When it's clear, you can see four states—Illinois, Indiana, Michigan, and Wisconsin."

The gift shop has all the Chicago souvenirs you'd ever want: maps, photo murals, T-shirts, postcards, coffee mugs, flags, pens. An instant-photo booth captures smiles against a city skyline for $3. Down the hall, wave hello to the people at Shadow Broadcasting who are announcing the latest traffic reports, sports, news, and weather information to radio and TV listeners.

The boy who was scared riding the elevator up is waiting at the exit sign. "Hey, Dad, can I walk down the stairs?" His father looks at me and rolls his eyes. *Michigan Avenue*

The John Hancock Center, 875 N. Michigan Ave., Chicago, IL 60611; (312) 751-3681. Hours: 9 a.m.-midnight. Admission: $3.25-$5.75. Indoor parking.

51 / Designer Boutique Where Service Is an Art

Henri Bendel

It's the little touches that count. For example, a huge circular mirror and a suede chair in the hat department, so you can try on hats in comfort. Or merino wool sweaters organized by color and stacked into a honeycomb wall shelf, so that a sweater is easily matched to slacks or a skirt.

I once brought in two pairs of prized slacks that needed new tops for an updated look. A Bendel stylist, looking like a hip version of Cleopatra, showed me to a spacious dressing room and proceeded to lug in trunkloads of exciting possibilities. An hour later, I was outfitted with two blouses, two jackets, and a snappy vest, all coordinated perfectly with the slacks, giving me six new outfits. It's the little touches that count.

Evening wear is sublime: black lace nothings that are everything, ball gowns to transform any Cinderella, beaded velvet strapless numbers.

There's nothing at Henri Bendel the well-dressed woman wouldn't crave. From fuzzy mohair sweaters to classic Italian suits, this store is about fashion that looks great on everyone. Yes, prices are high, but so is quality and style.

The first floor has a bazaar of fanciful costume jewelry, Italian and American leather handbags, luxurious scented candles, and makeup counters where stylists do complimentary makeovers. French fragrances waft from a tiny gold atrium in the back, in divine scents of tuberose, jasmine, and vanilla. Create your own personal perfume to go with your new look. Just another of Henri Bendel's little touches.

Michigan Avenue

Henri Bendel, 900 N. Michigan Ave., Chicago, IL 60611; (312) 642-0140. Hours: Monday-Saturday 10 a.m.-7 p.m., Thursday 10 a.m.-8 p.m., Sunday noon-7 p.m. Free Makeovers Monday-Saturday 11 a.m.-5 p.m. Reserve a week or two in advance.

52 / A Luxury Hotel in the Heart of Mag Mile

Four Seasons Hotel

"This morning I'm booking London theater tickets for a guest here in the hotel," smiles concierge Abigail Hart. "And I'm arranging dinner reservations in Paris, and obtaining opera tickets in Vienna." Ms. Hart also attends to the six phones at her desk that ring all day with other guest requests.

It's clear why the efficient Ms. Hart won 1994 Concierge of the Year from the prestigious Les Clefs d'Or: her Rolodex of world contacts and her gracious manner are one reason Four Seasons Hotel Chicago has won its third consecutive *Mobil Travel Guide* Five-Star Award.

The 343 luxuriously furnished guest rooms have city or lake views, overstuffed beds, and marble bathrooms. Rooms receive three inspections before a guest settles in.

Kids are treated to giant chocolate chip cookies, milk, and balloons in their rooms, and Fido is welcome, too. No doubt Ms. Hart has doggie treats available upon request.

The Health Club offers a stunning skylighted pool with city views, outdoor sun deck, running track, high-tech training equipment, whirlpool, sauna, and massage.

Stay cozy on a cold Chicago afternoon in front of the hotel's antique Italian marble fireplace, and enjoy a lunchtime pasta buffet. Or shop the 900 North Michigan Avenue Building the hotel shares with Bloomingdale's and 65 other international boutiques.

Michigan Avenue/North

Four Seasons Hotel, 120 E. Delaware Pl. at 900 N. Michigan Ave., Chicago, IL 60611; (312) 280-8800.

53 / A World of Fashion on One Eclectic Street

Oak Street Shops

On this street, people watching is serious entertainment: Revlon blondes in designer suits, ponytailed gents in khakis and Reeboks, slinky brunettes with tanned legs and pouty red lips, society women who dazzle in *Town and Country* party photos. Welcome to Oak Street—a lively neighborhood showcase for a world of beautiful fashions and decorative objects.

Brighten your outlook with a makeup makeover from Marilyn Miglin. Delight in couture from Giorgio Armani, Gianni Versace, Ultimo, and Sonia Rykiel. Don Eurochic eyewear from Optica. Sport a new Italian leather bag from Bottega Veneta. Get funky in fashions from Sugar Magnolia. Customize a gentleman's shirt from 600 different fabrics at Sulka, or select a luxurious cashmere bathrobe.

Surprise your groom at the altar in a divine silk gown from Ultimate Bride. Or rejuvenate through pampering from a sleek salon: Ilona of Hungary Skin Care Institute, Cote d'Or Coiffures, and Colin of London all offer the latest beauty tips and styles.

More recent arrivals on Oak Street include Jil Sander, fashion-forward German designs; Elements, unique gifts for the home; Hino and Malee, Chicago designers with an international flair; Stephane Kilian, French shoes; Pratesi Linens, the finest bedwear to dream on; Sansappelle, custom-designed evening wear; and Lester Lampert, fine jewelry and sensational designs inspired by the *Phantom of the Opera*.

Few streets have their own parking valet, but Oak Street does. Leave your car with Jon Farnick in front of 67 East Oak, and shop till you drop.

Michigan Avenue/Gold Coast

Oak Street Shops, Oak between Michigan Ave. and Rush St. Hours: 10 a.m.-6 p.m., Monday-Saturday, some stores open Sunday. Valet parking $7-$9.

54 / Delightful Gifts for Home and Friends

Branca Boutique

Never live without sunflowers again. At Branca Boutique they're freeze dried, blooming forever from moss-covered terra cotta pots.

"We're a lifestyle store," says manager Leslie Mader, "specializing in home furnishings, gifts, and decorative accessories."

Hypnotic potpourri lures you to fragrant shelves of crimson and pink baby rosebuds; dried oranges, apples, and nectarines; taupe and peach seashells; bath soaps and salts; body crème; and ornate candles. Vegetarians and chefs will love the dried jalapeño peppers and artichoke hearts sprinkled with chili oil.

"Every dog has his day" announces Branca's Dog Line of sports caps and ceramic snack bowls for Bowser. For pedigreed pooches, rubber chew toys are shaped like Queen Elizabeth crowns, and dog jackets are strictly designer. Sports dogs will appreciate red inflatable rubber bowls for family picnics.

The altar bound will be amused by "hopeless diamonds": Paul Bunyan-sized brass napkin rings with Elizabeth Taylor-sized "crystals." This is a great shower gift for a bride with a sense of humor.

More whimsy: wooden blocks imprinted with words like "wicked" and "dreaming," to help aspiring poets compose provocative poetry, cards titled "52 Tokens of Affection," and hilarious 1950s books with romantic advice including "Girls do not like to be asked for dates at the last minute." Men, take note.

Lime-colored glass decanters are topped with stars, moons, and hearts of cast iron. Pillows wish "May All Your Dreams Come True"; travel books suggest "Cheap Eats in Paris"; and framed antique prints sport graceful red tulips. Many gifts are under $50.

Owner Alessandra Branca and Manager Mader make frequent buying trips to Italy and France searching for the trendiest "cool stuff" to delight and decorate.   *Michigan Avenue/Gold Coast*

Branca Boutique, 944 N. Rush St., Chicago, IL 60611; (312) 664-4200. Hours: Monday-Saturday 10 a.m.-6 p.m., Sunday noon-5 p.m.

55 / An Art Deco Hotel on Chicago's Serene Gold Coast

Le Meridien Chicago

Nestled in Chicago's swank Gold Coast, an elegant neighborhood of vintage brownstones and tree-lined streets, is Le Meridien, an art deco-style hotel with 247 modern guestrooms. Billy Joel, Liza Minnelli, and Tina Turner stay here; so do honeymooners who book the Penthouse Suite, which features a spiral staircase curving to a king-size mauve bedroom and a balcony with views of Michigan Avenue.

Restful rooms have deep-turquoise carpets and black furnishings. Every room has three telephones, voice mail messaging, CD players and discs, and a remote-controlled stereo TV with built-in VCR. Bathrooms are roomy: enjoy oversized soaking tubs and separate glass shower stalls, terry cloth robes, fresh flowers, hair dryers, and a generous basket of amenities. Japanese guests are outfitted with yukatas and 24-hour room service menus in Japanese.

Other nice touches: Kathy Smith's workout tape and a step-exercise platform delivered to your room without charge; a shoehorn bigger than Texas in the closet so that you don't have to lean over to pull on your boots; and a fifth-floor vending machine that rents videos from *Forrest Gump* to *The Lion King*.

The Brasserie Bellevue Bistro is pretty, with ivory fabric draped from the ceiling and large sunny windows. Diners enjoy baked brie and lobster, smoked salmon, grilled lamb chops, and great people watching. Save that sweet tooth for the Saturday afternoon chocolate lovers' buffet.

Michigan Avenue/Gold Coast

Le Meridien Chicago, 21 E. Bellevue Pl., Chicago, IL 60611; (312) 266-2100. Room rates: $149-$700.

56 / An Upscale Jewish Deli on Chicago's Elegant Gold Coast

Winklestein's

Deli lovers rejoice. Indulge your dreams of cheeze blintzes, smoked sable, chicken soup with matzo balls, and hot pastrami adorned with chopped liver. Oy vey, you won't go hungry at Winklestein's.

Winklestein's built up a loyal clientele during their four-year stint in the River North area, then moved to the Gold Coast in late 1994. Dill pickle door handles give a fast clue to what awaits you inside: three dining areas, two fireplaces, and a coffee/cocktail bar.

Owners Scott and Steve DeGraff fell in love with Zingerman's deli in Ann Arbor during their college days at the University of Michigan. Deciding that Chicago needed a real Jewish deli, the brothers convinced their favorite cook, Suzie DeGraff, to share her superb Russian and Hungarian recipes with Chicago deli connoisseurs. Now the three partners are busy seven days a week, cooking up turkeys, corned beef, roast beef, brisket, baked goods, homemade soups, french fries, even homemade salad dressings.

Deli lovers study Winklestein's massive menu as though it were a stock market page. They face difficult decisions choosing from almost 100 sandwiches with names like "Good Golly Miss Molly" (hot pastrami or corned beef served between crisp latkes); "Bill's Big Bonanza" (smoked turkey, ham, gruyere cheese on rye); or "Pop's Nosh" (hot corned beef, chopped liver, Swiss cheese, cole slaw, and Russian dressing on an onion roll).

Besides the gargantuan selection of sandwiches, the menu includes fish, vegetarian plates, knishes, latkes, kugel, salads, a potato bar, low-fat/no-fat entrées, and at least five kinds of homemade soup. The chocolate peanut butter cup cookie, the rice pudding, and Winklestein's Jewish donuts (fried cinnamon raisin bagels dipped in cinnamon sugar) are worth the fat and calories.

Forget dieting, essen mein kinder.   *Gold Coast*

Winklestein's, 1120 N. State St., Chicago, IL 60610; (312) 642-3354. Hours: open 7 days 7 a.m-10 p.m.

57 / A Relaxing Coffeeshop among Vine-covered Mansions

The Third Coast Coffeehouse and Wine Bar

In the quiet residential Gold Coast neighborhood, business people and parents with toddlers and dogs in tow stroll past vine-covered mansions and gardens with red geraniums. Few escape the corner of Goethe and Dearborn, where heavenly aromas of espresso, cappuccino, latte, and café au lait lure the caffeine-addicted into a most enticing den.

Burgundy and blue upholstered banquettes line walls hung with black-and-white portraits. Handcarved wooden chess pieces wait to checkmate in front of sunny windows of beveled glass. Magazines and newspapers appeal to an eclectic readership: a 1957 issue of *True*, a 1960 issue of *Better Homes and Gardens*, and current issues of *New City: Chicago's News and Arts Weekly*.

Around the room people read, write, listen to quiet jazz, and gossip about who's doing what with whom. Some peruse a menu that offers eggs, pancakes, quiche, fruits, cereal, scones, muffins, soups, salads, sandwiches, and hearty fare such as beef stew and grilled chicken breast with couscous. The wine and beer list spans the globe.

There's no pressure to do anything except relax and hang out. Strangers often find themselves in conversation, but it's just as easy to retreat into a favorite book. *Strong Coffee*, a local newspaper of stories, poetry, and essays, catches my eye with a Zen reminder: "Time spent fishing is not deducted from the balance of one's life."

Neither is time at a swell Chicago coffeehouse.

Michigan Avenue/Gold Coast

The Third Coast Coffeehouse and Wine Bar, 1260 N. Dearborn St., Chicago, IL 60610; (312) 649-0730. Open 24 hours, 7 days a week.

58 / Chicago's Hippest Celebrity Nightclub Scene

Drink

Adorning the doorway: a steel sculpture of two curvaceous nude women happily guzzling big drinks.

"Things can get a little wild around here," laughs co-owner Scott DeGraff. "Gorgeous women dancing on the bar, movie stars showing up in limos. Michael Jordan usually stops by every few weeks for a drink with his chauffeur, George."

A Tribal Room has rope hammocks swinging from the ceiling. The Psychedelic Room has a vodka bar serving up strawberries and pineapples that have been swimming in Absolut for who-knows-how-long. It only takes one to feel absolutely psychedelic.

People watching is entertaining: models in little-nothing dresses, Miss Universe contestants, regular working women who happen to look like *Cosmo* covers, guys in tuxedos with sun glasses, and Bruce Willis types in torn blue jeans.

Drinks are served in purple and orange baby bottles with nipples and squatty plastic buckets with a straw. Who would think a baby bottle could be so hip?

Co-owners Scott DeGraff and Michael Morton, friends since fifth grade, opened Chicago's coolest nightclub in 1992 to great reviews. Besides the beautiful-people scene, Drink serves delicious food all day and into the night: petite filet mignon, rigatoni with artichoke hearts, Caesar salad with grilled chicken.

Music runs the gamut: reggae, funk, rock and roll. Revelers dance anywhere and everywhere—even on the bar.

"Drink is our clubhouse," smiles Scott, "a place where normal people can have a lot of fun. No harassment, no drunks, lots of security." And you don't even have to bring your own baby bottle.

River West

Drink, 541 W. Fulton St., Chicago, IL 60606; (312) 226-2555. Hours: Monday 11:30 p.m.-2:30 a.m., Tuesday-Friday 11:30 p.m.-4:00 a.m., Saturday 5:30 p.m.-5 a.m. Live concerts throughout the year. New Year's Eve party.

59 / Southern Italian Cuisine in Chicago's Gritty Warehouse District

Vivo

Tucked among a stark panorama of warehouses, water towers, and wholesale food markets is Vivo, a restaurant serving southern Italian cuisine with a distinctive style. Plates of colorful antipasti decorate a massive slab of polished granite near thousands of stacked wine bottles lining exposed brick walls. Tables and chairs bathed in streams of light are handmade. A twisting metal staircase leads to Vivo's most requested perch, a bird's-eye-view table for eight.

Chef Massimo Salatino and his team are on stage here, as the kitchen is open to allow guests a view. Salatino trained at Stresa, Italy's prestigious culinary institute, before working as a chef in Switzerland, France, Hawaii, and New York. Though he can no longer pick his own garden vegetables as he once did in his La Mezia, Italy backyard, Salatino shops each morning in the neighborhood for the freshest produce.

Many items on Vivo's menu are prepared on a wood-and-charcoal-burning grill, thus adding a fragrant aroma to the intimate restaurant. Antipasti change daily, offering marinated vegetables and rolled eggplant with prosciutto and mozzarella. Appetizers include carpaccio rustico, thinly sliced beef tenderloin with lemons, capers, and parmesan; and insalata di gamberetti con fagioli, grilled shrimp with a bean salad. Favorite entrées include orechiette pasta with broccoli in light garlic sauce, and roasted veal chops with artichokes and potatoes. Dessert highlights are tiramisu, crème brûlée, and fresh seasonal fruit.

"I like our open kitchen," says Chef Massimo, "because it gives me the opportunity to see how the food, the customers, and the atmosphere all mix together into something really unique."

River West

Vivo, 838 W. Randolph St., Chicago, IL 60607; (312) 733-3379. Hours: Dinner Monday-Thursday 5 p.m.-midnight, Friday-Saturday 5 p.m.-1 a.m., Sunday 4:30-11 p.m. Lunch Monday-Friday 11:30 a.m.-2:30 p.m.

60 / Eclectic Variety of International Art in One Neighborhood

The Gallery District

Within the River North neighborhood are dozens of outstanding galleries specializing in a variety of artistic expression. Many of the finest are members of the Chicago Art Dealers Association. Most are located on West Superior, West Huron, West Erie, North Orleans, Wells Street, and Franklin Avenue.

Gallery members of Chicago Art Dealers Association are: Aaron, Robert Henry Adams, Roy Boyd, Jan Cicero, Douglas Dawson, Catherine Edelman, Ehlers Caudill, Oskar Friedl, Kay Garvey, Richard Gray, Gruen, Gwenda Jay, Carl Hammer, Rhona Hoffman, Hokin Kaufman, R. S. Johnson, Douglas Kenyon, Phyllis Kind, Klein Art Works, Lydon Fine Art, Marx, Thomas McCormick, Mongerson-Wunderlich, Ann Nathan, Isobel Neal, Perimeter, Maya Polsky, Printworks, Lorenzo Rodriguez, Betsy Rosenfield, Esther Saks, Schneider Gallery, Space, Struve, Zaks, Zolla/Lieberman.

Information on specific exhibits and openings appears in two publications: *Art Now Gallery Guide* (monthly); and *Chicago Gallery News* (January, April, September), both available free at galleries, visitors' centers, and most major hotels. The Chicago Art Dealers Association will furnish current information on any of their members.

River North

Chicago Art Dealers Association, 107A W. Delaware Pl., Chicago, IL 60610; (312) 649-0065. Natalie van Straaten, Executive Director.

61 / Colorful Restaurant with Oprah's Famous Potatoes and Cookbook

The Eccentric

When The Eccentric opened in 1989, celebrity gazers flocked here hoping to glimpse the restaurant's most famous investor, talk-show hostess Oprah Winfrey. The most popular item on the menu was "Oprah's Potatoes," a spicy mashed-potato concoction that mom never thought of.

The Eccentric still serves some 300 pounds of "Oprah's Potatoes" every Saturday night, but everything else on the menu has changed since Executive Chef Jody Denton came aboard.

Some chefs learn their craft by studying at renowned cooking schools or working with other chefs. Chef Denton did that, but he also ate his way through an education. "First I was eating Indian food, then Thai, then Japanese," he laughs, "and reading every cookbook I could get my hands on. After years of eating and reading, I had a global encyclopedia of spices, herbs, and sauces. What I enjoy doing at The Eccentric is manipulating them into new dishes with flavor and flair."

A quick glance at the menu reveals some tempting combinations: Jamaican jerk chicken and black bean ravioli with mango relish and plantain chips. Sort of the gastronomical equivalent of Italian reggae.... Or how about grilled salmon with red-chili potatoes, mustard greens, roasted corn, and mint aioli?

Oprah's presence is strong. The restaurant's gift shop sells her newest cookbook, hats, T-shirts emblazoned with her portrait— even bowls for her famous potatoes. But the real reason to stop by The Eccentric is to enjoy a memorable meal from an innovative chef.

River North

The Eccentric, 159 W. Erie St., Chicago, IL 60610; (312) 787-8390. Hours: Lunch Monday-Friday 11:30 a.m.-2 p.m. Dinner Monday-Thursday 5:30-10 p.m., Friday-Saturday 5:30-11 p.m., Sunday 5-10 p.m. Entrées average $7.95 to $19.95.

62 / Italian Restaurant Celebrates the Beautiful People

I Tre Merli Restaurant and Bar

"I opened I Tre Merli because of the beautiful women in Chicago," grins co-owner Paolo Secondo, " and because you never know what's going to happen in this town. Maybe a Ferrari or a motorcycle will drive into the restaurant, or the customers will dance on the bar. Who can tell?"

The first I Tre Merli opened, in Genoa, Italy, back in 1978. Paolo and partner Pietro Pagano now have I Tre Merli restaurants in Miami Beach, in Soho, and at Trump Tower in New York.

"We're not here to cook spaghetti," Paolo says. "We're here for fashion, trendiness, design, the Italian style of life." Indeed guests here are very attractive, but the real stars are the food: grilled calamari with fresh herbs and lemons; seared tuna; salmon or beef carpaccio; penne with fresh artichokes and shrimp. I Tre Merli carries its own private-label fine wines, created for the restaurant by vineyards in the Piedmont region of Italy.

Chef Peter Graziano's culinary focus is on specialties of the Italian Riviera, such as grilled sea scallops with cannellini beans and fried leeks and fresh lobster and avocado salad. His zuccotto, vanilla and chocolate mousse with hazelnuts and chocolate chips in maraschino-liqueur sponge cake, is not to be missed.

The main room features 20-foot ceilings with skylights, a 35-foot-long bar, and thousands of wine bottles. One evening Paolo and Pietro hosted a beach party, trucking in tons of Lake Michigan sand. Guests padded around in bare feet, drank plenty of Champagne, and had a good time. Next morning, the sand was back where it belongs—along Lake Michigan.

As Paolo says, at I Tre Merli you never know what's going to happen next. *River North/River West*

I Tre Merli Restaurant and Bar, 316 W. Erie St., Chicago, IL 60610; (312) 266-3100. Hours: Monday-Thursday 11:30 a.m.-midnight, Friday 11:30-1 a.m., Saturday 5 p.m.-midnight, Sunday 5 p.m.-1 a.m. Entrées: $9.75-$19.75. Reservations suggested.

63 / Handmade Paper Inspiring Every Artist's Creativity

Paper Source

A bride-to-be carefully selects cream-colored paper from India, embedded with pale pink flower petals. "For my wedding invitations," she smiles.

A couple standing at the wall of wrapping papers debates sheets designed with cat tarot cards and cowboys on horseback.

"We specialize in handmade papers from around the world," says Paper Source manager Rebecca Dooddy. "If it's unusual, funky, or cool, we've got it."

Thousands of paper sheets are displayed on dozens of shelves. Some are embedded with fibers, parsley, rice, cinnamon, or slices of dollar bills. One is made with algae from a Venetian lagoon. You'll see every color in the rainbow and some new ones, too.

"People use them on tables and walls for decor, or make them into lampshades, box covers, menus, résumés, invitations, stationery. The limit is only your imagination," notes Rebecca.

Besides papers, the shop carries hundreds of rubber stamps: zebras, horses, raccoons, elephants, butterflies, wedding cakes, trumpeting angels, lacy hearts, sunflowers. Stamps remind readers "don't postpone joy," "remember mom," and "talk to Elvis, 1-900-The King." Choose a stamp pad in any color. Stamp your bills, your checks, or anything that stands still long enough.

Owner Susan Lindstrom inspires the artist in everyone by offering classes at the shop throughout the year. Learn to "create your own invitations" or "cover furniture with paper." Her own paper-covered chair, "upholstered" in red-speckled granite and French-marble papers, is a marvel to behold.

Textures, colors, designs are inspiring, so select a fabulous paper and a funky stamp and get creative.

River North

Paper Source, 232 W. Chicago Ave., Chicago, IL 60610; (312) 337-0798. Hours: Monday-Friday 10 a.m.-6 p.m., Saturday 10 a.m.-5 p.m., Sunday noon-4 p.m. Papers cost $2-$50.

64 / A Bookstore That Helps with Life's Transitions

Transitions Bookplace

Changing to a new job, a new home, or a new relationship can be very stressful. So a bookstore specializing in life transitions may be just what the doctor ordered.

"When you start to redefine a part of your life," says co-owner Gayle Seminara, "it causes you to re-evaluate other areas. Our store offers the opportunity to make changes and improve." Categories of books include health and healing, relationships, meditation, recovery, ecology, mythology, inspiration, fitness, nutrition, healthy cooking, and coping with grief.

Owners Howard Mandel and Gayle Seminara started Transitions from a 400-foot garage in 1989. Today their 5,800-square-foot bookstore in the bustling Clybourn neighborhood is an oasis of serenity. Soothing music and tiger lilies on café tables invite a relaxing book browse over a cup of lapsang souchang tea and raspberry ruggelah.

Gifts include a miniature Zen rock garden, complete with sand, tiny rocks, and a wooden rake for creating meditative designs; garnet and silver antique pendants from India, and jewel-toned journals emblazoned with "dancing ink" Chinese characters. Cards and T-shirts carry self-esteem and environmental messages, while cassettes and CDs offer contemplative harmonies. Reviews and author interviews are published in Transitions' complimentary quarterly newspaper, *Body, Mind, Spirit*.

"As adults we have the opportunity to continue growing," says Gayle. "Unlike our grandparents, we're not just worried about putting food on the table and a roof over our heads. We all can enhance the quality of our lives."

Clybourn

Transitions Bookplace, 1000 W. North Ave., Chicago, IL 60622; (312) 951-READ. Hours: 7 days, 9 a.m.-10 p.m.

65 / Risk-taking Award-winning Ensemble Theater

Steppenwolf Theatre Company

Chicago Tribune critic Richard Christiansen described one Steppenwolf production as "a brilliant kaleidoscopic rush of savage satire and deeply moving drama." *Chicago Sun-Times* theater critic Hedy Weiss lauded the company's "outstanding performances, including bursts of brilliance."

Steppenwolf has come far from the 1974 church basement in Highland Park where an ensemble of nine actors determined to create provocative theater. Actor and director John Malkovich, who joined Steppenwolf in 1976, once concluded a National Endowment for the Arts presentation by saying, "Look, you're either going to help us or you're not going to help us.... If you don't, we'll be here doing plays because that's what we want to do."

The company got its NEA grant and since 1979 has collected a dazzling array of prestigious production and performance awards, including Joseph Jeffersons, Emmys, Obies, Drama Desks, and several coveted Tonys. John Malkovich, Laurie Metcalf, Gary Sinese, John Mahoney, Gary Cole, and Frank Galati have established careers in TV and film as performers, writers, and directors. Director Galati's adaptation of John Steinbeck's *The Grapes of Wrath* won a 1990 Tony for Best Director and Best Play.

Producing works by Pinter, Caryl Churchill, Sam Shepard, Wallace Shawn, Chekhov, Wilder, and Williams, Steppenwolf has taken a number of shows to New York and Washington, as well as England and Australia. Steppenwolf's *The Song of Jacob Zulu*, featuring South African singing group Ladysmith Black Mambazo, was nominated for six Tony Awards.

"We're not afraid to go out on a limb," says *Zulu* director Eric Simonson. "Our emphasis is on acting, on exciting ensemble theater. At Steppenwolf, we're dedicated to what's new, bold, and controversial." *Halsted*

Steppenwolf Theatre Company, 1650 N. Halsted St., Chicago, IL 60614; (312) 335-1650.

66 / Spanish Tapas Restaurant with a Healthy Twist

Cafe Ba-Ba-Reeba!

A señora wearing a halo of grapes and bananas relaxes in a brightly colored hammock. A wall sign demanding, "No se paren," (don't stop) leads to a room where Crayola-gone-wild colors insist a party's going on.

"We're one big family here," says Cafe Ba-Ba-Reeba! chef Mark Tatschl, who at 6'5" is definitely the leader of the pack. "Our goal is to be in tune with the times, serving Spanish food that's full of flavor but not full of calories."

Chef Tatschl's menu makes it easy to enjoy tasty tapas-appetizer-sized dishes that won't throw you off a low-fat, low-calorie diet—as well as more traditional dishes. Try "ternera asada," cold roast veal with raspberry vinaigrette and oven-dried tomatoes. Or "salmon ahumado con patatas," smoked salmon with baby red potatoes and dill vinaigrette.

Tatschl remembers the dish that won him his job as executive chef: "Solomillo con cabrales," grilled beef tenderloin with Spanish blue cheese crust served on homemade garlic potato chips. He also recommends "chuletas de cordero," herb-and-mustard-crusted lamb chops served with pureed white beans and roasted garlic.

"I'm trying to create a happy balance between meat and potato lovers and health-conscious eaters," observes Tatschl, "presenting classic foods of Spain with an American twist."

A mural depicting Chicago's sculptures and politicians is signed Rambowski Picassowitz. The Cafe Ba-Ba-Reeba! message is clear: lighten up and enjoy. *Halsted*

Cafe Ba-Ba-Reeba!, 2024 N. Halsted St., Chicago, IL 60614: (312) 935-5000. Hours: Lunch Tuesday-Saturday 11:30 a.m.-2:30 p.m., Dinner Monday-Thursday 5:30-11 p.m., Friday 5:30 p.m.-midnight, Saturday 5 p.m.-midnight, Sunday noon-10 p.m. Entrées range from $5.50 to $15.95.

67 / Unique Art and Gifts for Home and Office

Jayson Gallery

Mauve and cream pillows made from kilim rugs are piled high in an antique bathtub with claw feet. Oak and pine armoires display handblown glass pens and ceramic retro vases. Sleek photo frames float images in textured glass or surround them with stainless-steel rivets. Miniature books on music, flowers, wine, and food are inexpensive gifts, as are coasters printed to look like computer circuit boards. Handblown glass vases show off curvy shapes and serving platters come in 1950s gold, cornflower blue, or pea green. Photo albums are wrapped in leather, wood, and bright kilim tapestry.

Jayson's merchandise-unique, whimsical, and romantic—includes intimate books of classic "lover" photos titled *For You* and handmade silkscreened anniversary cards.

Halsted/Clybourn

Jayson Gallery, 1915 N. Clybourn Ave., Chicago, IL 60614: (312) 525-3100. Hours: Monday-Friday 9 a.m.-6 p.m., Thursday 9 a.m.-8 p.m., Saturday 10 a.m.-5 p.m. Gifts $10 and up.

68 / Tapas Restaurant with a Sizzling Salsa Dance Band

Bossa Nova

A lady in red shares a pitcher of sangria with her equally seductive friends. Hot white light streams onto swank bar tables where two lovers whisper. Speakers vibrate with salsa, jazz, and reggae.

On this Wednesday evening it's only 7 p.m. but already Bossa Nova is heating up. By 8:30 the tables are filled, and the live "world-beat" band lures diners onto the tiny dance floor. Who can stay seated when working off calories is this much fun?

Bossa Nova's menu, created by chef David Del Gatto, features a diverse selection of tapas inspired by Mediterranean and PanAsian cuisines. "We offer a variety of tapas to stimulate every taste and appetite," says Del Gatto. "Bossa Nova is an international food experience."

Three tapas per person easily make a satisfying meal. Seared tuna rolled in black pepper and sesame seeds, served in a butter-soy sauce with tender noodles on the side, melts in your mouth. Grilled Jamaican jerk chicken in a peppery sauce of honey and scotch-bonnet chilies is juicy. Blackened scallops, charred crispy on the outside and soft and sweet inside, are bathed in a butter-and-wine sauce with lime juice, shallots, and parsley.

Vegetarians enjoy chilled fresh spinach tossed with sesame and tomato chunks. "Ribs from Hell" with chipotle barbecue sauce are fall-off-the-bone tender.

Tapas are complemented with wine from Chile, Australia, Italy, or California; imported beers; and Champagnes. Creamy chocolate-banana gelato is the perfect dessert.

The night is young, the band is live. Put down that fork, get up, and dance. *Halsted/Clybourn*

Bossa Nova, 1960 N. Clybourn Ave., Chicago, IL 60614; (312) 248-4800. Live music: Wednesday-Saturday 8:30 p.m.-11 p.m., Friday 10:30 p.m. on, Saturday 11:00 p.m. on. Tapas average $4.95-$6.95, entrées from $10.95 to $14.95. Reservations suggested.

69 / Boutique for Confident, Fashionwise Women

Wear in Good Health

Chicago designers Julie Felps and Laurie Ledford originally opened this tiny boutique to sell clothes they designed. "We've expanded to offer other designers as well," says manager Rebekah Wiest, "like Diesel Italian jeans, French Connection suits, and Susie Tompkins dresses."

Clothes at this tiny boutique are for the woman who's proud of her size 4, 6, or 8 well-exercised curves. If you tend toward khaki pants and Reeboks, this is not your kind of clothing store.

Do you have the confidence to don a brown leather mini-skirt and matching bomber jacket? Or a petite black lycra T-shirt worn over a short flared skating skirt? Sexy slip dresses are another option; choose from black, pink, banana, and moss green.

Black is the main fashion color here in dresses, pants, and sweaters, but everything is cut to celebrate a womanly shape. Diesel jeans are sleek fitting in soft periwinkle blue. French Connection pants suits in cornflower blue and burgundy could go to work, but teamed with a sexy lace camisole, look great for dancing or dining.

Hats are funky, slouchy, or Annie Hall adorable. Accessories include suede belts, sunglasses, and textured stockings. Tiny glass beads make earrings delicate.

With the Gypsy Kings playing softly in the background, and the low-key help of Rebekah and assistant manager Maureen McInerney, Wear in Good Health is a pleasant place to re-discover feminine allure.

Halsted/Clybourn

Wear in Good Health, 2204 N. Clybourn Ave., Chicago, IL 60614; (312) 929-0883. Hours: Monday-Friday 11 a.m.-7 p.m., Thursday 11 a.m.-8 p.m., Saturday 10 a.m.-6 p.m., Sunday noon-5 p.m.

70 / Interactive Museum Where Chicago History Comes Alive

Chicago Historical Society

"Children find Chicago history fascinating," says Barbara Parson, a Chicago Historical Society interpreter of nine years. "The pioneers, Indians, Great Fire—all are exciting for them to hear about. How we overcame our problems is what Chicago's spirit is all about."

At the Historical Society, the city's history unfolds in all its dimensions: high culture, everyday life, ground-breaking architecture, brawny politics. From railroads to meat packing, steel, Tootsie Rolls, and bicycles, the museum showcases artifacts that make history come alive.

"We the People: Creating a New Nation" presents the stories of extraordinary people during the Revolutionary War and the nation's early years. "A House Divided: America in the Age of Lincoln" reveals the pivotal role of slavery in dividing America and how the country finally resolved the issue.

In "Hands-On History Gallery" kids can walk into an early fur trader's cabin, browse through old Sears catalogs, ride a highwheel bicycle, recreate the sounds of a 1930s radio show, and play with 19th-century toys.

Special events—walking tours, storytelling, a children's film festival—are scheduled regularly throughout the year. Mrs. Parson says there are some kids on her tours who burn with important historical questions. "Just the other day," she recalled, "a girl from Japan asked me 'what's the difference between Chicago pizza and regular?'

"Chicago pizza is thicker," explained Mrs. Parson.

At the Chicago Historical Society, no question goes unanswered. *Lincoln Park*

Chicago Historical Society, 1601 N. Clark St. (at North Ave.), Chicago, IL 60614; (312) 642-4600. Hours: Monday-Saturday 9:30 a.m.-4:40 p.m., Sunday noon-5 p.m. Admission: $1-$3. Free Mondays.

71 / Hip Western Wear with Quality Jewelry, Clothes, Furniture

Out of the West

Then there was the time a city slicker strutted in looking for cowboy boots to match his Cadillac. Seems his 1958 beauty was Pepto-Bismol pink and tar black, and the urban cowboy thought matching cowboy boots would finish off his look. No problem. Just another day at Chicago's hippest western outfitter.

When the front door is a horse corral and the welcome mat says "Howdy," you know this is not just another chain store.

Start with the basics: chino pants, a cotton T, and a plaid shirt designed by Ralph Lauren. Add a silver-buckle belt from Wyoming and a pair of handmade boots from Texas or Mexico, and you're ready.

How about sprucing up your homestead with handmade couches, chairs, and desks? And don't you need that iron chandelier: buffalo and steer dancing around a handpainted rawhide teepee. That coyote-skull pipe might work over the fireplace.

Out of the West also sells leather-bound journals; Navaho rugs; funky photo frames; and enough turquoise earrings, necklaces, watches, and rings to outfit your whole tribe. Miniature gift books are by Edward S. Curtis, who spent his life photographing indigenous peoples for his 20-volume work, *The North American Indian*.

The store window displays a buffalo-sized Indian motorcycle for sale. Interested in trading your horse?

Lincoln Park

Out of the West, 1000 W. Armitage Ave., Chicago, IL 60614; (312) 404-9378. Hours: Monday-Friday 10 a.m.-8 p.m., Saturday 10 a.m.-7 p.m., Sunday 11 a.m.-5 p.m.

72 / Chic Designer Clothes for Savvy Businessmen

Bigsby & Kruthers

Why do sports heroes, TV newscasters, actors, politicians, and CEOs shop here? First let's flash back to 1970, when Joe and Gene Silverberg pooled their cash and opened a store selling army surplus goods and jeans. When a Gap store down the street offered competition, they decided that "upscale" was their arena. The Silverbergs bought 1,000 Pierre Cardin suits from a factory in Colombia and—presto—exit surplus, enter swank.

By 1984, the Silverbergs had published their first *Suit Book,* a hip photo collection of Chicago celebrities clad in elegant B & K attire. Bigsby & Kruthers was immortalized as the store of choice for guys with clout.

Today the *Suit Book* features actress Marlee Matlin, Bulls player B. J. Armstrong, "NYPD Blues'" star Dennis Franz, actor Joe Mantegna, and Hyatt Chair Darryl Hartley Leonard.

With six Chicago locations and an ever-increasing number of Knot Shop stores, a nationwide chain selling men's fashion neckwear and accessories, the sky's the limit. The Silverbergs have already won Esquire magazine's "Top Five Clothiers in the Nation," and have joined the ranks of *Who's Who in Chicago Business*.

"We've grown up with our customers," says Gene Silverberg. "They trust us to guide them up to the edge of what they can wear to the office without going over the boundaries. In business and socially, clothes are a man's passport. In the Bigsby & Kruthers movie, the man gets the promotion *and* the girl."

Lincoln Park

Bigsby & Kruthers, 1750 N. Clark St., Chicago, IL 60614; (312) 440-1700. Hours: Monday 11 a.m.-9 p.m.; Tuesday-Wednesday 10 a.m.-8 p.m.; Thursday 10 a.m.-9 p.m.; Friday-Saturday 10 a.m.-6 p.m.; Sunday noon-5 p.m. Offers shoe shine, barbershop, manicurist, and Bigsby's Bar & Grill.

73 / Lincoln Park's Most Romantic Restaurant and Nightclub

Toulouse on the Park and Toulouse Cognac Bar

Owner Bob Djahanguiri has surrounded himself with goddesses. His elegant Lincoln Park restaurant sports a jewel-embossed ceiling; crimson velvet upholstered banquettes; and fanciful murals of nubile goddesses celebrating food, wine, and song.

"My goal was not only to create a restaurant with outstanding food and service," he explains, "but just the right setting for love." Lovers are treated to specials such as steamed artichoke with sherry, sautéed shrimp with sweet-and-sour sauce, saddle of venison, grilled quail, roasted rack of lamb, or a fragrant bouillabaisse of Australian prawns, whitefish, tuna, snapper, and scallops.

Having hosted family parties as a teenager in Iran, studied engineering at the University of Oklahoma, and dined at many of the world's five-star restaurants, the imaginative Mr. Djahanguiri has created an opulent love nest where passion is part of the evening.

After dinner, in the intimate Toulouse Cognac Bar across the hall, couples cuddle around the gleaming ebony baby grand, listening to "I Love Paris," "Get Happy," and "Embraceable You." Cognac and music go down easy any night, with top Chicago artists such as Dave Green, Audrey Morris, Nan Mason, and Frank D'Rone. Monday evenings jazz treasures Johnny Frigo and Joe Vito take requests for "Try to Remember," and "I'll Be Seeing You." One stroke of his electric violin and you know why Mr. Frigo won a Chicago Music Award in 1994 as Best Musician and Best Jazz Artist. Here are songs that engage heart and soul from music makers who know what romance is about.

Lincoln Park

Toulouse on the Park and Toulouse Cognac Bar, 2140 N. Lincoln Park West, Chicago, IL 60614; restaurant (312) 665-9071, bar (312) 665-9073. Restaurant: Monday-Thursday 5-10:30 p.m., Friday-Saturday 5-11:30 p.m. Cognac Bar: Monday-Thursday 8 p.m.-1 a.m., Friday 6 p.m.-1 a.m., Saturday 6 p.m.-2 a.m.

74 / Zoo Home to U.S.'s Largest Lowland Gorilla Family

Lincoln Park Zoo

Not many zoos sponsor gorilla film festivals. Last summer, zoo fans were treated to an evening starring Bushman, Otto, Sinbad, Koundo, and other famous Lincoln Park Zoo apes. What—you've never heard of these guys?

Lincoln Park Zoo is home to the largest collection of captive lowland gorillas in the United States. Since 1970, 38 gorillas have been born at the zoo. There's always some kind of party going on here: Zooperbowl in January, Run for the Zoo and Zoorobics in June, a bluegrass Country Fair in July, Spooky Zoo Spectacular in October, and Caroling to the Animals in December.

Stop by and visit Sikhote and Bransk, two handsome six-year-old Siberian tiger brothers who took up residence at the zoo in 1993. They've joined the zoo's other 1,600 animals, including birds and reptiles, from every corner of the globe. Nearly 30 endangered species are among the species represented. Gorillas, orangutans, chimpanzees, elephants, rhinos, hippos, wolves, giraffes, flamingos, mynah birds, polar bears, big cats, penguins, seabirds, gibbons, camels, zebras, gazelles, and koalas—all await your visit.

Kevin Bell, Director of Lincoln Park Zoo, grew up visiting New York's Zoological Park, where he was described as "the boy with 2,081 pets." He became Lincoln Park Zoo's Curator of Birds at age 23 and oversaw the renovation and construction of all the zoo's bird areas. His conservation work has taken him to Panama, India, Africa, and Iceland. His efforts in Indonesia releasing Bali Mynah birds back into their native habitat has helped increase the number of these birds from fewer than 20 to 35.

Say hello to the Zoo's two Bali Mynah birds, where they have a very safe Chicago home. *Lincoln Park*

Lincoln Park Zoo, 2200 N. Cannon Dr., Chicago, IL 60614; (312) 935-6700. Open daily, 9 a.m.-5 p.m. Free admission. Call for schedule of events.

75 / Inspiring Continental Cuisine in a Romantic Setting

Ambria

Few Chicago restaurants have celebrated their fifteen-year anniversary with four-star reviews from *Chicago Magazine*, the *Chicago Tribune*, and the *Mobil Travel Guide*. Ambria deserves the accolades.

An elegant art nouveau decor of deep-toned woods, tiny shaded table lamps, and crystalline etched glass creates an ambience in which slowly savoring one's food and company is an entire evening's activity. The attentive staff encourages a relaxed mood by not overwhelming diners with excess information about the preparation and ingredients of every dish on the menu. They assume you can make your own decisions and wait patiently until you do so.

Fortunately the menu is not gargantuan. Takashi Yagihashi, chef de cuisine, has reduced the former menu, which listed 13 appetizers and 14 entrées, to a more manageable 9 appetizers and 11 entrées. "My goal is to create simple dishes that are executed well," he says. 'What's most important is the flavor and texture, as well as the presentation."

Chef Yagihashi reveals some of his most popular entrées: carpaccio of tuna and yellow tail with Oriental vinaigrette, baby pheasant with wild mushrooms and thyme broth, loin of lamb with sweet mini peppers, and breast of Muscovy duck with spring potatoes. "Not too many flavors," he cautions, "just the natural juices and light sauces for best enjoyment."

Save room for delicious desserts created by pastry chef Cindy Cameron: dessert soufflés with Grand Marnier; banana mousse with caramelized banana and chocolate; chocolate euphoria, a milk-chocolate mousse cake.

Lincoln Park

Ambria, 2300 N. Lincoln Park West, Chicago, IL 60614; (312) 472-0076. Hours: Monday-Thursday 6-9:30 p.m., Friday-Saturday 6-10:30 p.m. Entrées: $19.50-$29.95. Valet parking.

76 / Greenhouse Garden of Brazilian, African, Asian Plants

Lincoln Park Conservatory

In this magical indoor garden, it's always summer. Coconut palms, rubber trees, and tropical plants from Brazil, Ethiopia, and China stretch several stories high. Hot, moist air is a sweet-smelling Earth fragrance. Classical piano music blends with the splash of mini-waterfalls.

"If you want to remove yourself from the daily grind, this is where to find peace and serenity," says Sopie Nardi, a floriculturist with Chicago's Park District for more than 18 years. Like a doting grandmother, Ms. Nardi sees to the well-being of her floral grand-children.

Wander into the fern room, a sunken glade that is home to cycads, one of the oldest known plants. Bird's nest ferns have upright fronds arranged in perfect nests, and familiar Boston ferns recall 1970s home and restaurant decor. Plant names are in Latin, for example, *cyntonium falcatum Rochefordianum Polypodiaceae.*

Stone steps curve gracefully up to the cactus room, an arid sandy desert where cacti from Brazil and Zimbabwe reach thorny arms to skylight windows. New Mexico's cholla grows here, as well as Mexico's fishhook and cowhorn from Cape Province.

"A couple in their 80s came to the conservatory from Scotland," Ms. Nardi fondly remembers. "They had fallen in love here 65 years ago and wanted to relive their courtship days."

Meanwhile, across the street in his own romantic oasis, a watchful statue of William Shakespeare keeps an eye on new lovers.

Lincoln Park

Lincoln Park Conservatory, 2400 N. Stockton Dr., Chicago, IL 60614; (312) 294-4770. Hours: daily 10 a.m.-5 p.m. Free admission.

77 / Cozy Café Serves Homemade Breakfast and Dessert All Day

Ina's Kitchen

Were you one of those kids whose parents never had time to cook? Do you remember years of cold, mushy cereal and half-frozen TV dinners?

Go to Ina's, she'll take care of you.

Huge blueberries nestle on fluffy pancakes. Fresh fruit and lemon zest adorn thick slices of French toast. Real maple syrup floods whole-wheat oatmeal pancakes. Vegetable hash cozies up with two poached eggs. Larger-than-life omelettes overflow with herbed cheese, spinach, bacon, or mushrooms. Eat, be happy.

Having been in the bakery business for over ten years, "I know sugar, flour, and eggs," laughs Ina. "It's natural for me to create nurturing, comforting breakfast food. And since breakfast is my favorite time, we serve it all day."

The salmon-pink and sky-blue walls are a perfect backdrop for the relaxed Lincoln Park crowd of businesspeople, volunteers, and women on "the mommy track." Diners talk, laugh, and linger over a third cup of fresh-ground coffee. Floor-to-ceiling windows admit sunshine, views of grocery stores and vintage brownstones.

If you want something other than breakfast, order a lunch special such as spinach egg soup, marinated lentil salad, or cold Chinese noodles with crispy peapods. There are also side dishes of potatoes, scrapple, bacon, veal-chive sausage, and that all-time kid favorite, peanut butter sandwiches.

Ina's homemade cakes are not to be missed: devil's food, carrot, banana toffee, pumpkin cheesecake. Or try nut torte, peach tart, or key lime pie—made the way your mother never had time for.

Ina has time for everyone. So join her for breakfast, even if it's lunchtime. *Lincoln Park*

Ina's Kitchen, 934 W. Webster St., Chicago, IL 60614; (312) 525-1116. Hours: breakfast, lunch Tuesday-Friday 7 a.m.-3 p.m., Saturday-Sunday 8 a.m.-3 p.m. Entrées: $4.25-$7.25. Special-order cakes average $21.

78 / Comfortable Bed and Breakfast in Serene Lincoln Park

Bed and Breakfast Lincoln Park/Sheffield

As exciting as Chicago is, the noise and craziness can overwhelm even the most enthusiastic traveler. Here's a lovely, residential neighborhood bed and breakfast where peace and quiet abound. Sheffield is a pretty street of turn-of-the-century houses, chic boutiques, ethnic restaurants, coffee houses, and funky gift shops.

Chicago's downtown Loop is just two miles south; Lincoln Park Zoo, the Chicago Historical Society, and Lake Michigan are an enjoyable 20-minute walk east.

Three types of accommodations are available. The Owner's Bedroom has a black-lacquer Ming Dynasty four-poster bed, huge closets, private bath, huge living room, and use of a contemporary white kitchen. Eat at the countertop, or relax on the couch.

Another room is the Honeymoon suite, which has two bedrooms (in case of an argument?); a private bath; and a galley kitchen with refrigerator, stove, sink, microwave, and dishwasher.

A third possibility, the Master Suite, is a cozy English basement with a living room, private bath, double bed, and sleeper sofa. Though it has no kitchen, there is a small refrigerator, microwave, and toaster oven for late night-snacks.

Each unit has cable TV, telephone, answering machine, and coffeemaker. Breakfasts offer a choice of fresh bagels, croissants, or sweet rolls, fresh fruit on request, cereal, coffee or tea, and orange juice.

"What I love about running a B & B," says owner Elia Sandoval, "is meeting wonderful people and helping them enjoy Chicago." Blackie and Sheba, her black Labrador retrievers, enjoy houseguests as well.

Lincoln Park

Bed and Breakfast Lincoln Park/Sheffield, 2022 N. Sheffield Ave., Chicago, IL 60614; (312) 327-6546. Rates: $65-$145, two-night minimum. Parking available, $5 per day with advance reservation.

79 / Delightful Books and Events for the Kid in Everyone

The Children's Bookstore

Next to an overstuffed reading chair, a six-foot-tall rabbit wears ballet shoes and a pink tutu. Potter, a live rabbit, hops among kids browsing through their favorite books. Store manager Andrew Laties, who looks like a kid with a beard, dashes about preparing for the Peter Rabbit vegetable hunt. In a few hours, hundreds of delighted children will be running amok, combing the store for hundreds of carrots, potatoes, and radishes.

It's just another day at Chicago's most innovative children's bookstore, where 25,000 titles await discovery. The store catalogue features book reviews by Chicago-area children. Kelly Dunleavy, a fourth grader from Pilgrim Lutheran School, read *Chocolate Fever* by Robert Kimmel Smith, "because my sister eats a lot of chocolate and I wanted to know what would happen."

In addition to books, there's an interesting selection of educational toys, games, and puzzles. Super Optic Wonder is a popular science toy, combining a compass, binoculars, flashlight, Morse code, and magnifying glass. Young artists enjoy the face painting kit where they colorize their little mugs into clowns, tigers, and ship, captains. Noncompetitive games "help kids learn to enjoy cooperation and helpfulness" says Laties, pointing out Eyes of the Jungle, in which players act as park rangers, helping to restore endangered species to their natural habitats.

Special events occur almost daily, and range from story hours, singalongs and pajama parties to performances by children's choirs and folksingers. A parade of authors, performers, and storytellers makes for a bookstore where adults have as much fun as children. Potter the rabbit loves company.

Lincoln Park

The Children's Bookstore, 2465 N. Lincoln Ave., Chicago, IL 60614; (312) 248-2665. Hours: Monday-Saturday 10 a.m.-7 p.m., Sunday 11 a.m.-6 p.m. Story hours Tuesday-Thursday 10:30-11:15 a.m.

80 / A 1950s Diner Serving Up Burgers, Shakes, and Elvis

Johnny Rockets

"When I applied here for my job as a waitress," says Esperanza Hernandez, "the staff were all dancing." This spic-and-span shiny 1950s diner revs up everyone's happy feet. Customers drop coins into countertop mini-jukeboxes and out blasts "Twist and Shout," You Ain't Nothing But a Hound Dog," and "Respect."

Maybe it's the nostalgic decor: a blue, pink, and black Formica counter surrounded by cherry red swivel stools and *Life* magazine covers of baby-faced Frank Sinatra. Must be the fresh food: thick, made-to-order hamburgers, grilled and served with lettuce, tomato, mustard, pickle, onion, mayo, and relish.

"One customer drove his blue Mercedes right up to the door one night," laughs manager Renee Moore, "and came in dancing to the music, shouting 'Gimme a chocolate shake to go.' We get lots of customers like that."

Johnny Rockets concocts a shake to die for: fresh, hand-dipped ice cream blended with whole milk, real fruit, and syrup, served with a melting mound of whipped cream in a tall glass. Luscious slurps are worth the calories.

The staff is a friendly group that calls regulars by their first names. Johnny Rockets Restaurants are found in Australia, Canada, England, Japan, and Mexico, as well as twelve states in the U.S.

So when your kids are ready for adventures beyond the golden arches, "twist and shout" at Johnny Rockets for homemade burgers and heavenly shakes.

Lincoln Park

Johnny Rockets, 2530 N. Clark St., Chicago, IL 60614; (312) 472-6191. Hours: Sunday-Thursday 7 a.m.-midnight, Friday and Saturday 7-2 a.m. Entrée prices: $2.95-$3.45.

81 / The Midwest's Largest Ceramic Shop & Gallery

Lill Street Gallery

Inside the converted horse and carriage barn there's a sign announcing "playful forms, painterly surfaces, a celebration of functional ceramic and surface decoration."

Founded in 1975 as an artists' cooperative, Lill Street is the midwest's largest ceramic center, with a gallery and shop featuring work by over 200 local and national artists. Some forty-five artists call Lill Street their working home, creating innovative ceramics upstairs in private studios and classrooms.

With the exposed brick walls, high ceiling, and soothing classical music, Lill Street is a relaxing space to browse for the unusual. Oversized ceramic bowls are emblazoned with pink tiger lilies, luscious peaches, and ready-to-cook eggplants. Shelves show off Greek, Italian, Southwestern, and Oriental-style ceramics, such as an urn covered with colored glass mosaic; portraits of swimming fish; and an amazing array of fanciful teapots.

Guest curator and ceramics artist Kelly Kessler says Lill Street has carved a niche with "new trends in pottery—items that are functional and enduring, but also inventive, fun to use, and sometimes whimsical."

The gallery's jewelry and gift shop brims with delicate earrings, papier-mâché finger puppets, wooden toy rabbits and alligators, and ceramic cat pins.

Classes for adults and children are always going on, as are one-day workshops. In June and August, and during the winter holidays, it has an art camp for kids 5-14. The gallery also hosts children's birthday parties for which Lill Street provides the teacher, supplies, goody bags, and classroom. You bring food, kids, and creativity.

Lincoln Park

Lill Street Gallery, 1021 W. Lill Ave., Chicago, IL 60614; (312) 477-6185. Gallery hours: Tuesday-Saturday 11 a.m.-6 p.m., Thursday until 8 p.m., Sunday noon-5 p.m. Call for class and events schedules.

82 / Tattoo Parlor with Thousands of Provocative Designs

Chicago Tattooing Company

Tattoo artist David McNair turns the shoulder of a suburban hairstylist into a bouquet of scarlet roses. Wearing latex gloves, he dips a sanitized needle into thumb-sized pots of red and green paint, and less than an hour later the customer is smiling in front of the mirror, admiring her new tattoo. "Pretty sexy," she says.

At the counter, a couple of candidates page through the design book trying to choose from butterflies, skeletons, eagles, and fire-breathing dragons. Wrap a slithering snake around an ankle, fly a winged unicorn across a shoulder, or check out the latest body painting creations in *Tattoo Magazine*.

"Over half of our customers are women ages 21 to 30," says graphics designer Jim Ronan. "They come in for something to remember Chicago by. And we get plenty of doctors and lawyers, not just sailors and bikers," he laughs.

Ronan has created thousands of designs over the years, some so pretty you might think about using them for wallpaper in your favorite room. Flowers, vines, curving lattices, and hearts abound. Ronan says career tattoos are popular: hairstylists come in for scissors, plumbers ask for monkey wrenches, and carpenters like hammers. Other folks bring in photos of their cats and dogs or illustrations of tigers and bears. Sometimes there are odd requests like a skull with nine daggers in it. Whatever you want, you get.

Prices run from $20 for a name or a small heart up to $3,000 for a full back tattoo in living color. Walk-ins are fine; but you must be 21 or older to get a tattoo.

David McNair's business card says it all: "Chicago's oldest and finest; realistic, energetic work that speaks for itself."

Lakeview

Chicago Tattooing Company, 922 W. Belmont Ave., Chicago, IL 60657; (312) 528-6969. Monday-Saturday noon-10 p.m., Sunday 2-6 p.m.

83 / Authentic Mexican Restaurant in a Bohemian Neighborhood

Mi Tierra

Belmont Avenue is a schizophrenic street: you have to cover your ears against the roaring El and pounding jackhammers, avoid people with shaved heads and rings in their noses, and step over people sitting on the sidewalk talking to themselves. A chain doughnut shop makes a handy corner hangout near shops offering riveted leather jackets, red lace bustiers, and flavored condoms.

Then there's Mi Tierra, a sweet little Mexican restaurant where paper cutouts of pineapples and flowers hang over tables covered with green and red tablecloths like a child's birthday party. Framed oil paintings romanticize Mexican countrysides and villages at sunset.

Obviously the owners have turned their backs on the madness of the world outside in favor of the memory of "mi tierra" (my land). Young waitresses with long hair, white lace blouses, and bright red lipstick make dining recommendations in English or Spanish.

Start out with the chips and salsa. We guarantee you'll want to take home a jar of Mi Tierra's special salsa.

Move on to the guacamole. Shrimp fajitas, tiny fresh shrimps grilled with onions, tomatoes, and bell peppers, arrive with side orders of rice, beans, and a small salad. Other favorites are Mexican pepper steak; chilies rellenos; chicken in mole sauce; and red snapper breaded and smothered in a spicy tomato sauce.

These dishes from Jalisco tend to be lighter than the food from some other regions of Mexico. Even the obligatory rice and beans are light and flavorful, and the corn tortillas are homemade.

After seventeen years on wild and crazy Belmont Avenue, Mi Tierra is still a welcome oasis in a crowded urban landscape.

Lakeview

Mi Tierra, 1039 W. Belmont Ave., Chicago, IL 60657; (312) 929-7955. Hours: Monday-Friday 10:30 a.m.-midnight, Saturday-Sunday 10-2 a.m. Entrées range from $5.75 to $8.

84 / Ivy-covered Home of the Chicago Cubs

Wrigley Field

Driving west to 1060 Addison, you know you've arrived in Chicago Cubs territory: bars, parking lots, hot dog stands, and gas stations all proclaim the team's latest victory or mourn its latest defeat. After 119 National League seasons and over 17,397 games, few teams are more loved or hated than the Cubs.

For you trivia buffs, we've assembled some important Wrigley Field/Chicago Cubs facts. Built in 1914, Wrigley Field is the third-oldest ballpark in the major leagues, behind Detroit's Tiger Stadium and Boston's Fenway Park. Originally, Wrigley Field was called Weeghman Park and was build on grounds once occupied by a seminary. The park name was changed to Wrigley Field in 1926 in honor of William Wrigley, Jr., the club's owner. In 1981 the club was purchased by the Tribune Company.

Weeghman Park was home to the Chicago Whales of the short-lived Federal League. The first National League game at the ballpark was played on April 20, 1916, when the Cubs beat the Cincinnati Reds 7 to 6 in 11 innings.

Historic moments of note: Babe Ruth's "called shot," when the Babe allegedly pointed to a bleacher location and hit Charlie Root's next pitch in that vicinity for a home run on October 1, 1932, during Game 3 of the World Series. There's Ernie Banks's 500th career home run on May 12, 1970, against Atlanta's Pat Jarvis. And Pete Rose's 4,919st career hit, which tied him with Ty Cobb for the most hits in baseball history.

After much heated debate, Wrigley Field finally added lights for night games in 1988, the last major league ballpark to do so.

One last thing: What was the team's original 1876 name?

The "White Stockings," of course. We know you knew.

Lakeview

Wrigley Field, 1060 W. Addison St., Chicago, IL 60613; (312) 404-CUBS. Purchase tickets by mail, at the Wrigley Field ticket office, or call (312) 831-CUBS.

85 / Sports Outfitter for Water, Snow, and Rollerblade Fans

Windward Sports

Two curvaceous girls in black spandex tops and shorts cruise in on rollerblades. A muscular dude stands before eight styles of sailboards trying to decide which will carry him farthest fastest.

If you're into sports—as a participant, not as a spectator—this is the place to gear up: snowboards, skateboards, surfboards, boogieboards. And look for the right look: sexy, shiny bikinis; sleek one-piece suits for serious swimming; leather fanny packs; flannel shirts; jeans; vests; teva sandals; fleece sweatshirts; microplex snowsuits; caps that say "eat or be eaten." Dive skins as pink and turquoise as Caribbean parrotfish.

"Whether your sport is on the beach or in the snow, we can outfit you for windsurfing, rollerblading, snowboarding, and skateboarding," says store manager Jackie Butzen, svelte, tanned, and athletic looking.

Windward Sports is Chicago's only sports-gear store that carries surfboards, windboards, snowboards, and custom skateboards. The skateboards are displayed on the basement wall like modern art, with images of beach babes, heavy metal guitars, killer fish, and leering boys from the hood. A TV monitor over the rollerblade service counter runs tapes of California dudes who make rollerblading up brick walls look normal.

Lakeview

Windward Sports, 3317 N. Clark St., Chicago, IL 60657; (312) 472-6868. Hours: Saturday-Monday 10 a.m.-5 p.m., Wednesday-Friday 10 a.m.-8 p.m.

86 / Superb Japanese Sushi, Seafood
Matsuya

The people waiting in line are hugging, laughing, and introducing friends and family to each other. No one seems to mind waiting for one of the 40 tables in this crowded, noisy neighborhood restaurant. Steaming bowls of rice go by, followed by black lacquer trays laden with artfully designed sushi. Large blue plates overflow with tempura shrimp and vegetables. The pungent soy sauce aroma and the Japanese music make waiting bearable.

The wall menu looks like a handmade billboard, announcing today's fresh rainbow trout, red snapper, butterfish, kingfish, mackerel, and grouper. Special appetizers include soft-shell crab, fresh soybean, seaweed salad, and spicy scallops.

Families and couples, about half of them of Asian descent, sit elbow to elbow toasting over giant bottles of Kirin beer and mugs of steaming tea. African Americans with waist-length cornrows sit next to tattooed women with nose rings and kids wearing Bulls caps backwards. Matsuya's simple, serene decor includes gleaming wooden tables, shoji windows, and fresh crimson gladioluses curving out of a woven basket.

Finally we dive into our own feast: fried soft-shell crab that is light and crunchy; broiled eel on rice; chicken teriyaki with sesame seeds; sunomo, thinly sliced cucumber in vinegar dressing; and Osaka-style sushi, thick slices of salmon, mackerel, and tuna on large squares of sticky rice.

During dinner there's a power outage, and the entire restaurant goes dark. People keep eating and talking, the line of people waiting to eat stays just as long, and one group bursts out into a rousing Kirin-induced version of "Happy Birthday" to all of us.

For dessert we can't decide between green tea ice cream and "homemade fruit jello." We skip both. We've already discovered what the menu promised: "a truly wonderful experience for both eye and taste." *Lakeview*

Matsuya, 3469 N. Clark St., Chicago, IL 60657; (312) 248-2677. Entrées: $8-$17.

87 / Delicious Fare in an Intimate Bucktown Rowhouse

Jane's

Inside this unpretentious Bucktown rowhouse are soaring ceilings; 3-D paintings of lemons, limes, and strawberries; and huge bunches of gladioluses.

Diners are an eclectic group: businesspeople in funky outfits, parents with toddlers, video production crews, actress wannabes, and construction workers wearing hard hats.

One freeway worker eats at Jane's every day because "I'm a vegetarian, I'm picky what I eat, and they take the boring out of vegetables."

Behind the bar is the kitchen, no bigger than a ship's galley. Chef Tony Recillas and co-owner Jeff Auld are a blur, cooking for today's hungry lunch bunch. They boil, broil, sautée, bake, and grill together like old-time dance partners. Jeff is lean and intense. Tony is laid back and has an "isn't this craziness fun" grin.

Together the duo turns out some very flavorful fare: homemade corn chowder, in which the corn and carrots are actually crunchy and the potato chunks tender; South African fruit and vegetable curry that is spicy, sweet, and rich; hot sesame noodles that are both chewy and light. Favorite entrées include the garden burger, a veggie burger made with organic ingredients and served on a five-grain bun with gorgonzola and veggie bacon; and the Chinese chicken salad, a heavenly mixture of baby lettuces, won tons, carrots, cabbage, scallions, chow mein noodles, roasted cashews, and peanuts all tossed in a dressing whose ingredients are secret. Best dessert: homemade, not-too-sweet mixed berry pie.

Co-owner Arden Nelson is hostess and fairy godmother, seeing that her guests are relaxed and well fed. No problem. Jane's is as homey as eating at grandma's, except that grandma never cooked like this. *Bucktown/WickerPark*

Jane's, 1655 W. Cortland Ave., Chicago, IL 60622; (312) 862-JANE. Entrées: $6.95-$9.95; sandwiches average $5.95. Hours: 11 -1 a.m. 7 days a week.

88 / Old-fashioned Ice Cream Parlor Decadence

Margie's Ice Cream and Chocolates

Were you one of those kids who only ate dinner to get to dessert? In this old-fashioned ice cream parlor you and the kids can indulge sweet fantasies.

Seating about seventy, Margie's is a hodgepodge of stuffed animals, dolls, and boxes of homemade chocolates, all crammed into a Salvation Army decor of 1920s advertisements, juke boxes, and fake plants. But hip decor is not what Margie's is about, and nothing here is fat free.

Over in the corner, a family with twins is silent, completely absorbed in "terrapin sundaes," mounds of French vanilla ice cream lathered with thick homemade caramel and fudge sauce, chopped nuts, whipped cream, a red cherry, and, for that extra sugar boost, a cookie on the side.

Margie, who is 70-something, greets regulars by first name and newcomers as "honey." Maybe she'll invite you to sign her chocolate-stained guest book, where fans have penned reactions like "confectionery orgasm" and "Margie, can I get married here?"

Margie says vanilla ice cream is the most popular, but she also serves homemade chocolate, strawberry, pineapple, raspberry, blueberry, cherry, coconut, peach, chocolate mint, fudge, peanut butter, and banana. There's regular food such as tuna sandwiches and meat loaf, but why bother? Head straight for dessert, just like you wanted to way back when.

Bucktown/Wicker Park

Margie's Ice Cream and Chocolates, 1960 N. Western Ave., Chicago IL 60647; (312) 384-1035. Hours: 10 a.m.-midnight, 7 days a week.

89 / Sizzling Latin American Dance Club/Restaurant

De Cache

Hips swaying, shoulders proud, eyes locked, these couples can dance: salsa, merengue, cubia, tango. Whatever Orquesta Fuego bangs out on timbales, bongos, congas, trumpets, and trombones is embraced by this crowd with passion and style. It's too loud to talk, but why talk when the music is this hypnotic?

"You can feel our music from your feet to your head," says Orquesta Fuego's director Ray Cortez. "Beautiful rhythmic sounds that make you wanna get up and dance." Tonight the crowd goes wild over "Porque Te Amo" ("Why I Love You") and "Attración Fatal" ("Fatal Attraction").

At De Cache, Chicago's largest Latino entertainment center, it's always dance night. Wednesday is "Tropi-Salsa Night," with dance contests and raffles; Thursday is "Community Appreciation Night," with three bands and a free buffet; Friday night there's a free mambo class; Saturday night, strut your stuff at the mambo contest from which winners walk away with Champagne, concert tickets, and $1,000 cash prizes; Sunday features "Family Night," with mariachi bands and a free Mexican buffet.

"We attract a very elegant, international crowd," says General Manager Edgardo Lopez. "They live in Chicago, but are originally from Mexico, Colombia, Puerto Rico, Cuba, the Dominican Republic, Ecuador, Venezuela, Guatemala, Panama, and Argentina. And of course Anglos are welcome, too."

If you've yearned to dance Latin style, come see how the pros do it.

Bucktown/Wicker Park

De Cache, 2047 N. Milwaukee Ave., Chicago, IL 60647; (312) 489-9600. Hours: Monday-Thursday 8 p.m.-3 a.m., Friday-Saturday 8 p.m.-5 a.m. Admission: $5, ladies free until 11 p.m.

90 / Authentic Vietnamese Cuisine on the Magnificent Mile

Pasteur

Owner-manager Kim Nguyen never dreamed she'd be running one of Chicago's most popular Vietnamese restaurants. "My brother Tuan and I were traveling around the United States managing Vietnamese bands and singers," she recalls. "When we got to Chicago in 1985, we bought a restaurant, and that's how Pasteur got started."

At first they served only beef noodle soup to their mostly Vietnamese customers. But soon local magazines and TV stations pronounced Pasteur "the best Vietnamese food in town," and the menu and the crowds grew dramatically.

"We still use Vietnamese ingredients like our fish sauce, nuoc mam," says Kim, "but we combine them with French, Chinese, and Western cuisine as well. We want to introduce our visitors to new tastes they can't get anywhere else."

Favorite dishes include sliced beef marinated in lemon grass, sesame seeds, and oyster sauce, then grilled and served with soft rice paper, mint, cucumber, and bean sprouts. Spring rolls are marvelous: fresh shrimp, vegetables, and rice noodles rolled in rice paper, served with plum sauce, roasted peanuts, and shredded carrots. Shrimp and basil leaves served on a skewer with scallion and tomato sauce are picture-perfect and delicious.

Huge windows with pots of jade trees; honey-colored, wood-paneled walls; and watercolors of Hue, Vietnam create an airy atmosphere. Dress is casual, and you're apt to hear customers chatting in Vietnamese and Chinese, as well as English.

"We love to cook dishes to our customers' desires," smiles Kim, who at 28 may be the youngest restaurant owner and manager in Chicago. At Pasteur, diners enjoy every bite.

Downtown

Pasteur, 45 Chicago Ave., Chicago, IL 60611; (312) 271-6673. Hours: Monday-Thursday 11 a.m.-10 p.m.; Friday-Saturday 11 a.m.-11 p.m.; closed Sunday. Entrées $5.50-$10.50.

91 / Chinese and Taiwanese Specialties

Mei Shung

The decor of most mom-and-pop Chinese restaurants consists of little more than green linoleum floors and plastic tables. Mei Shung has created a serene atmosphere where horses fly across huge golden fans spread against pale gray walls. Delicate blue-and-white porcelain vases display pink silk cherry blossoms. An ebony screen, with inlaid mother-of-pearl creates two alcoves within the one-room restaurant. Manager Jean Kao, elegant in a linen suit, sees to her guests' comfort, stopping at every table to ask "How is the food; is it OK?"

Mei Shung is slightly off the beaten track of Argyle Street's cluster of enticing Asian restaurants and thus makes a big effort to attract diners with attentive service and a choice of menus: an extensive one with dishes from all over China and a smaller one with Taiwanese specialties.

Seasonal specials are also offered, such as soft-shell crab, which is served crispy and fresh in bite-sized portions accompanied by a decorative radish carved into a red rose. Mu shu pork, a standard Chinese dish of shredded pork sautéed with vegetables served wrapped in a Mandarin pancake with scallions and hoisin sauce, is delicious in Mei Shung's spicy version with homemade pancakes.

Kung bao chicken, diced chicken stir-fried with peanuts, bamboo shoots, water chestnuts, and scorched red peppers, has a spicy crunchy quality, helping an otherwise bland dish come alive. Shrimp fried noodles are satisfying, consisting of tender homemade noodles and very fresh shrimp cooked just before serving.

Watermelon, orange slices, and crumbly almond cookies refresh for dessert. Chocolate fortune cookies predict "a stranger will soon become your friend."

Andersonville/Argyle

Mei Shung, 5511 N. Broadway Ave., Chicago, IL 60640; (312) 728-5778. Hours: Tuesday-Thursday 11:30 a.m.-10 p.m., Friday 11:30 a.m.-11 p.m., Saturday noon-11 p.m., Sunday 3-9:30 p.m. Entrées: $5.15-$13.95.

92 / Distinctive Flowers, Delicious Ice Cream in a Historic Building

Anna Held Flower Shop and Fountain Café

The pink Edgewater Beach Apartments create a surprise exclamation point at the end of Lake Shore Drive. Built in 1928, the apartments were once next door to the Edgewater Beach Hotel, where well-heeled Chicagoans dined and danced under the stars. The hotel is gone, but the Edgewater Beach Apartments were awarded Historic Landmark status in 1994.

Anna Held Flower Shop and Fountain Café in the Edgewater is an oasis of flowers, gifts, and homemade desserts. "I was delighted to discover the 1920s Italian marble soda fountain," says owner Beth Tarrant. "And since original owner Anna Held operated the shop well into her 90s as a prominent floral designer, I decided to continue what she began."

Beth has succeeded, offering artistically designed arrangements with flowers like French tulips and Hawaiian birds-of-paradise. As a graduate of Chicago's School of the Art Institute, and a master of Japanese ikebana, Beth's philosophy is to "create nature for urban environments."

The beautiful marble soda fountain is a fun spot to indulge in Beth's homemade carrot cake, apple pie, and brownies. Many fall prey to hot fudge sundaes made with Sherman's Ice Cream, or Chicago-style chocolate phosphates, an irresistible mix of soda water, whipped cream, and ice cream.

The shop carries a potpourri of gifts, such as picture frames, miniature books, vases, and beeswax candles. Kids prefer the pocket frogs, finger puppets, and mobiles. A large selection of cards yields the perfect message for every occasion.

In a high-tech world of Internet and voice mail, it's comforting to indulge in the nostalgic delights of Anna Held's good old days.

Edgewater

Anna Held Flower Shop and Fountain Café, 5557 N. Sheridan Rd., Chicago, IL 60640; (312) 561-1940. Hours: Monday-Saturday 10 a.m.-6 p.m., Sunday 10 a.m.-4 p.m.

93 / Walk-in Yoga and Meditation Classes

Sivananda Yoga Vendanta Center

One block from a frenzied intersection of cars, trucks, buses, and taxi cabs is a little wooden house with blue trim. Inside there is no furniture. A hand-lettered sign on the wall requests, "Blessed students please leave your shoes on the left side of the stairs. OM."

Leave your stress, anxiety, and cramped muscles there too, because you're about to enter the world of Sivananda Yoga. The International Sivananda Yoga Vedanta Centers were founded in 1959 by Swami Vishnu-Devananda as a nonprofit spiritual organization whose purpose is to share "ancient yoga teachings as a means of achieving physical, mental, and spiritual well being."

Classes are held in large, carpeted rooms and start with deep breathing relaxation exercises. Then come "asanas," intense stretching of the knees, legs, and back. Time seems suspended. There are no clocks, no jarring music, just the sound of breath and heartbeats. The instructor's tone is soothing and encouraging. Many people go through the class with closed eyes to avoid distraction. There are no mirrors, no feeling of being watched or judged, no one to compete with.

Swami Sivananda's tenets are simple: "Lead a simple life. Practice daily meditation and establish peace in your own heart. Then you will radiate peace to all who come in contact with you."

Andersonville

Sivananda Yoga Vedanta Center, 1246 W. Bryn Mawr Ave., Chicago, IL 60660; (312) 878-7771. Hours: 10:30 a.m.-6:30 p.m.; open classes every day except Friday. First open class is free.

94 / Persian Cuisine with Family Ambience

Reza's Restaurant

It's noisy and the waiters are frantic, but if you don't mind dining with 400 other people, Reza's has delicious Persian and vegetarian cuisines.

The setting: a dark wooden ceiling, metal chairs upholstered with black Naugahyde, photos of Middle Eastern villages on the red brick walls. The bar is interesting, curving dramatically under a skylight, with what seems like thousands of Italian, French, and American wines nestled into the back wall.

The mostly family crowd is eclectic. Everyone comes to enjoy enormous portions of lamb kabob; chicken koubideh; broiled salmon; and domeh felfel, sweet green peppers stuffed with spinach or mushrooms. The vegetarian sampler is excellent for group grazing: dolmeh, shami, kashkeh bademjan, tabbouleh, hummus, rice. If you want to know what they are, don't ask the waiter, just order. It's terrific.

There are some offbeat items such as grilled catfish, juicy quail, and game hen with pomegranate sauce. All entrées are served with pita bread, parsley, feta cheese, radishes, onions, and bowls of tasty lentil soup. Reza's herbed basmati rice with dill and beans gives rice a whole new personality.

Desserts are sticky sweet and include zoulbia, a crisp, deep-fried pastry drowning in syrup, as well as baklava. Top them off with strong coffee that will keep you awake for the rest of your life.

Bring an appetite and a big party. Expect to take home tomorrow's lunch.

Andersonville

Reza's Restaurant, 5255 N. Clark St., Chicago, IL 60640; (312) 561-1898. Hours: daily 11 a.m.-midnight. Entrées: $5.25-$12.95.

95 / Eclectic Gallery of Art by American Women

Woman Wild

"We were inspired to name our store Woman Wild because author Sonia Johnson's book *Wild Fire* speaks of the creative energy of women, no matter what form it takes," says co-owner Janet Soule.

The store vibrates with the color and energy created by the 125 American women artists whose work is displayed. Themes are repeated in various media: woman as goddess, beauty of nature, respect for wildlife, exploration of fantasy, and dreams. Relaxed clothing sports images of floating balloons; picture frames are adorned with whole seashells, turquoise serving trays embrace flying dolphins, sleeping lizards, and flying horses. Rose-colored wine glasses are etched with serene mountain landscapes.

Next to each artist's work is a biography and a personal statement about her creative process. Gretchen Lima, creator of gypsy woman dolls, says "dollmaking has become an inner journey and a process of healing and self-empowerment."

Sculptor Julie Morrison says "my work translates my dreams and fantasies into an art form that has a life of its own…. With each piece created, a new dream is achieved."

Jewelry is one-of-a-kind at Woman Wild, in sterling silver, bronze, copper, and gold. Bracelets are layered with bronze and copper and inlaid with garnets and amethysts. Earrings feature cut-out buffalo silhouettes.

"Many women artists have difficulty making the transition from hobbyists to businesswomen," notes Janet. "At Woman Wild we give them a place in the market, encouraging them to go forward as artists."

Andersonville

Woman Wild, 5237 N. Clark St., Chicago, IL 60640; (312) 878-0300. Hours: 11 a.m.-6 p.m., Friday until 8 p.m.

96 / Diverse Books by, for, and about Women

Women and Children First Bookstore

On a given evening you might be treated to a reading by Alice Walker, Erica Jong, or Anna Quindlen. Lines of book lovers have wrapped around the block to hear Gloria Steinem, Adrienne Rich, and Margaret Atwood.

"We're a feminist and children's bookstore," says co-owner Linda Bubon, "featuring fiction, poetry, and art books by women, and nonfiction about all aspects of women's lives."

These shelves invite serious browsing and are stocked with books on women's studies (*American Women in the '90s*), spirituality (*Ask Your Angels*), biography (*Simone de Beauvoir*), psychology (*Women and Their Fathers*), and child care (*Feeding with Love and Good Sense*). There are also sections on gay and lesbian topics, multicultural issues, and general fiction.

Videos run the gamut from *Frida Kahlo* to *Thelma and Louise*, and T-shirts feature messages like "No Guilt." CDs and cassettes of music by women include k. d. lang and Sweet Honey in the Rock. The card selection is creative and extensive. There's also a nice selection of jewelry made by women.

Since children are first here, too, there are hundreds of books for kids of all ages, from picture books to books on insects and dinosaurs for preteens. On Wednesday mornings at 10:30, the bookstore hosts "Kiddielit for City Kids," a morning of lively stories, fingerplays, and silly poems for 2-4-year-olds.

Besides the very popular celebrity author readings, Women and Children First presents readings by emerging local writers. There are writing workshops and discussions on women's issues like self-image, food, and family.

Andersonville

Women and Children First Bookstore, 5233 N. Clark St., Chicago, IL 60640; (312) 769-9299. Hours: Monday-Tuesday 11 a.m.-7 p.m., Wednesday-Friday 11 a.m.-9 p.m., Saturday 10 a.m.-7 p.m., Sunday 11 a.m.-6 p.m. Call for a calendar of events.

97 / Coffeeshop/Bookstore/Boutique for World Travelers

Kopi: A Traveller's Café

When Rhonda Welbel and Karen Weinstock fell in love with Indonesia, they had no idea that someday, back in Chicago, they'd create a traveler's café.

"Throughout our own travel, we discovered that cafés are the ideal place to meet new people and share experiences anywhere in the world," says Rhonda, "so we've created a haven here where people can sit and refuel."

Kopi, Indonesian for coffee, is filled with travelers who come to read, write postcards, and exchange notes and ideas. Tables are hand painted with images of Greece, travel lists, and song lyrics. A backpacker relaxes among piles of guidebooks and maps. In the front window, two women sit cross-legged on colorful Moroccan pillows writing in their journals.

Rhonda and Karen opened Kopi in 1991. They pride themselves on serving coffee that is locally roasted and ground fresh daily and make their own house blend. Vegetarian sandwiches and decadent pastries—lemon poppyseed cake, for one—fill out the menu.

Wall shelves beckon with hundreds of travel guides for sale. A tiny boutique in the back corner overflows with international goodies: necklaces made of Chinese snuff boxes, Javanese glass beads, Moroccan rosewater flasks, Indonesian batik sarongs, vests from Guatemala and Turkey, buffalo-hide shadow puppets from Java. Carved wooden angels and dragons from Bali hang from the ceiling.

On the wall overhead, Kopi's clocks keep track of time in Moscow, Goa, Kathmandu, Yogyakarta, Denpasar, Kyoto, Alice Springs, and Rotorua. In Chicago it's time for coffee and talk of adventures still dreamed about. *Andersonville*

Kopi: A Traveller's Café, 5317 N. Clark St., Chicago, IL 60640; (312) 989-KOPI. Hours: Monday-Thursday 8 a.m.-11 p.m., Sunday 10 a.m.-11 p.m., Friday 8 a.m.-midnight, Saturday 9 a.m.-midnight. Occasional live music.

98 / Vegetarian Indian Restaurant in Little India

Udupi Palace

Devon Avenue is one of Chicago's more exotic streets. Kamdar Plaza advertises saris, spices, sweets, and snacks. Bombay Video features the latest Indian video stars, and the windows of Sari Sapne offer saris in cobalt, amethyst, and emerald chiffon, swiss voile, and buttersilk at two for $25.

Inside the Udupi Palace restaurant, middle-aged Indian women wear traditional saris to dinner, while their teen daughters and sons sport modern shorts and T-shirts. Grandparents keep a watchful eye over sleeping infants as a steady stream of fragrant vegetarian dishes emerges from the kitchen.

"Besides being strictly vegetarian," explains co-owner J. H. Khatwani, "we specialize in cuisine from southern India, near the area of Madras. The restaurant is named after the Indian town of Udupi."

For first-timers, the Udupi Special at $9.99 is a good beginner's guide: sample spicy Mulligatawny soup, a vegetable broth made deep yellow by pungent curry; vegetable uthappam, a seven-inch circular pancake embedded with tomatoes, peas, carrots, onions, and chilies; iddly, steamed rice and lentil dumplings dipped into onion curry sauce; and masala dosai, a crescent-shaped crepe overflowing the plate, brown and crispy outside, filled with tender onion and potato inside.

For a welcome relief from all the spice, for dessert have mango ice cream, which tastes like creamy butter; and masala tea—milky, fragrant, and strong.

The waitresses are Russian, the customers Indian and American, and the food is extremely filling and reasonably priced. This is the perfect place to wear your sari.

Rogers Park

Udupi Palace, 2543 W. Devon Ave., Chicago, IL 60659; (312) 338-2152. Hours: noon-10 p.m., 7 days. Entrées: $3.99-$10.99.

99 / Music, Dining Alfresco under Summer Stars

Ravinia

George Gershwin performed at Ravinia back in 1936 and raved, "A more delightful spot for a concert I cannot imagine." On a modern note, Itzhak Perlman thinks Ravinia is "one of the great festivals in America."

How can it miss? The roofed stage is open to the summer air, the green lawn invites picnics by candlelight, and the diversity of stars and programs is mind-boggling. Here's a sample of what Ravinia offered in summer 1994: the one and only Ray Charles; vocalists Zap Mamma, with blues and Babanzele pygmy chants; flamenco guitarist Paco de Lucia; sax player David Sanborn; John Denver; Tony Bennett; and Placido Domingo conducting Tchaikovsky's "Romeo and Juliet" with the Chicago Symphony.

Some nights are hotter than others: Los Lobos unleashes its Latino style of rock, Leny Andrade blends Brazilian samba and jazz, the Silk and Bamboo Ensemble performs music of China, and the Soweto String Ensemble mades its Midwest debut with African melodies.

Ravinia doesn't forget the kids either: there are morning and afternoon concerts with Fred Penner, star of Nickelodeon; "Sesame Street's" Bob McGrath; and singer-guitarist Tom Chapin.

Dining alfresco on the lawn is popular, and you can enjoy your own picnic. But you may want to dine at one of Ravinia's many restaurants: American harvest buffet at the Rondo, elegant indoor dining at The Cadenza, fried chicken from Counterpoint, burgers from La Grille, or cappuccino ice cream from La Cremerie. For six or more, you can call ahead for a catered dinner of cold shrimp, beef tenderloin, fried chicken, pasta salad, and dessert.

Summer stars on the stage and in the sky, a gourmet picnic to boot. What could be more relaxing? *Out of Town/North Shore*

Ravinia, Green Bay and Lake-Cook rds., Highland Park, IL 60035; (312) RAVINIA. Free park 'n' ride shuttle service for cars; bus and train service from downtown Chicago.

100 / Lush Botanic Gardens, Greenhouses, Special Plant Events

Chicago Botanic Gardens

Just 25 miles north of Chicago, an oasis beckons. Leave the four-lane highway (1-94 at Lake-Cook Road). Stop and smell the roses. The Botanic Gardens' 300 acres of rolling hills, native prairies, and 20 different gardens are a much-needed escape from Chicago's concrete jungle.

Pink and white water lilies bloom in a lush aquatic garden; 5,000 rose bushes perfume the air. Water cascades over shiny brown stones into gentle pools. The heritage garden, modeled after Europe's first botanic garden, in Padua, Italy exhibits plants in four quadrants, while the English walled garden unveils six "rooms" of artfully designed flowers and shrubs. Native Illinois plants thrive in the naturalistic garden, near a rolling sea of grass in the prairie garden.

My favorite, the Sansho-en Japanese garden, is a "garden of three islands," evoking serenity and harmony with nature.

Each garden unfolds new beauty as the seasons change. In winter visitors amble through tropical rainforests and arid deserts inside the greenhouses. The Education Center's garden shop offers horticultural supplies for those with green thumbs and classes for fledgling gardeners. In between tours and classes, Food for Thought Café serves tasty sandwiches, tempting desserts, and a varied choice of beverages.

Summer is the busiest season, with special events including June's National Peony Show, July's Daylily Show, and August's Midwest Bonsai Show. A narrated tram tour running throughout the gardens is a good orientation, as are the Monday evening carillon concerts in summer. Cooking classes are often held on the fruit and vegetable island, a tranquil Eden where gardeners become chefs. *Out of Town/North Shore*

Chicago Botanic Gardens, Lake-Cook Rd., Glencoe, IL 60022; (708) 835-5440. Open every day of the year except Christmas, from 8 a.m.-sunset. Admission free; parking $4.

101 / A Suburban Museum Inspiring and Delighting Children

Kohl Children's Museum

Compelling portraits of children from around the world decorate the walls. Amid pools of spotlights, voices of children call out: "Priviet!" "Dziendobry!" "Shalom!" "Hola!" Banners proclaim, "Beautiful people come in all colors" and "You can shape your future." Children nestle in a corner alcove, listening and singing: "If I were you and you were me, I'd care about your dignity, so let's share the world in harmony, as if I were you and you were me."

At Kohl Children's Museum, kids enhance their understanding of themselves and the world around them through multicultural experiences, problem solving, and role playing. The idea is to inspire children, parents, and teachers to discover new ways of learning through imagination, creativity, and fun.

Kids are going wild with fun here: climbing aboard a reconstruction of a CTA train for an imaginary ride downtown, discovering ways to conserve resources at the Recycle Center, traveling on a Phoenician sailing ship into an ancient royal kingdom, creating works of art, painting yellow and green daisies on their faces! Young shoppers push carts through a kid-sized grocery store as they learn to select healthful food for the family.

Founded in 1985, the Kohl Children's Museum was built on the success of its predecessor, the Kohl Teacher Center, a pioneer Chicago resource for over one million educators. Today the museum welcomes more than 250,000 visitors each year and has an extensive outreach program in the public schools.

If you can't find your kids, they're probably in the museum shop, stocking up on the latest educational toys, books, and games.

Out of Town/North Shore

Kohl Children's Museum, 165 Green Bay Rd., Wilmette, IL 60091; (708) 256-6056. Hours: Tuesday-Sunday 10 a.m.-5 p.m. Closed Monday. Admission: $2.50-$3; children younger than one are free.

Index

Notes

101 Great Choices